OUTSIDERS AND APPARITIONS

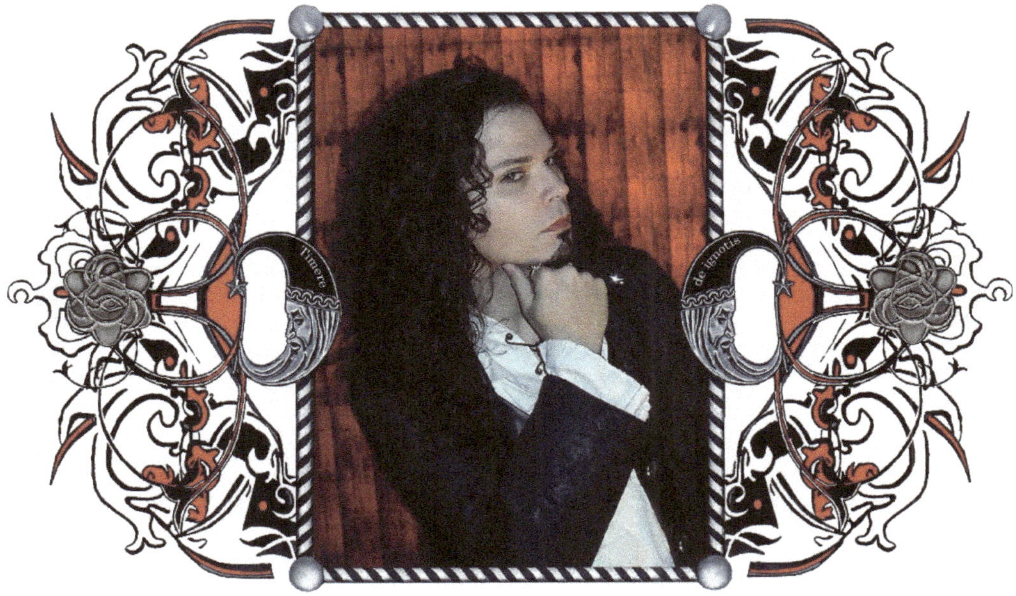

POSSESSED POEMS AND ART FOR FAMILY PICNICS

MILAN SERGENT

Praise for
Outsiders and Apparitions
Possessed Poems and Art for Family Picnics

"This superb collection of poetry and art, Outsiders and Apparitions by Milan Sergent, cleverly confronts societal opinions on outward success, happiness, and inner fulfillment.... Each poem is illustrated with the most extraordinary and exceptional artwork. I was absolutely captivated by this collection. Milan is such an inspirational artist and writer. His talent for provoking thought and change in human behavior is superb...."
—Lesley Jones for *Readers' Favorite*

"This is the best book of poetry that I have read this year. I absolutely enjoyed the ingenious poetry that Sergent brought to life in this collection.... What I loved even more was the collection of paintings that accompanied each poem.... Overall, I think Milan Sergent has created a masterpiece.... It's definitely a collection I would recommend. I can't wait to read more of his work."
—Tiffany Ferrell for *Readers' Favorite*

"[A] fabulous combination of art and poems that are unique, fresh, and unconventional and take readers to another realm altogether.... The collection is eclectic, unapologetic, and fantastical, and is a good way to make readers break free from their traditional ways of expressing themselves and to try out something different."
—Mamta Madhavan for *Readers' Favorite*

"Sergent brings a unique brand of surrealism to an emotionally resonant space in this collection, which explores personal and wider themes that play with structure and form in poetry, but also express a breakout from the conventions of language, art, and society.... Having been an ardent fan of Milan Sergent's fiction work for quite some time now, it was a delight to explore another facet of the author's mind and see his artistic process come to light in new forms.... Outsiders and Apparitions is a book that no poetry fan should be without."
—K.C. Finn for *Readers' Favorite*

"Milan Sergent's Outsiders and Apparitions is a collection of poetry and artwork that has a way of digging into almost all of your senses. His poetry has a lyrical, children's nursery rhyme sort of bent, but with an adult flavor and tone. An antiquated essence also paints every page, so that there is a feeling of transportation that takes us centuries back into the past."
—Erin Nicole Cochran for *Readers' Favorite*

To every person who has been rejected by family or who has felt like an outsider. To every person who was wrongfully killed.

Published by Cryptic Quill Publishing LLC.

ISBN 13: 978-1-7348775-5-7

Library of Congress Control Number: 2020920023

Contents

ATLAS OF CANDICE ... 1
A REALLY CLOSE SHAVE ... 3
HOCKING UP THE CLOCK TONIGHT ... 5
ADORING FANS ... 7
AGRICULTURAL ANGELOPHANY ... 9
CIRCULAR CREDO ... 11
DEATH AMONG THE LIVING ... 13
EMERGE ... 15
FAIRIES ... 17
I.C.U. ... 19
FALLUCINATIONS ... 21
SOME TALES ARE FLUFFIER THAN OTHERS ... 23
CHEAPER BY THE DOZEN - THE UNYOKING OF THE GOLDEN EGG ... 25
FATE'S FICKLE FINGER ... 27
FROSTED PHENOMENON ... 29
DEADHEAD THE DANDELIONS ... 31
UNDERNEATH MODEST DAYWEAR IS THE EVENING'S LEATHER AND DARE ... 33
ONLY DEATH SURVIVES ... 35
FUSIHATCHI'S OOKY DAY ... 37
GO TO THE LIGHT ... 39
MORTAL MORSEL'S DOMINION ... 41
LOLLIES ... 43
MADAME DACTYLIC ... 45
HEARTS ON STRINGS ... 47
HOW MRS. CLAUS LOST IT ALL ... 49
THE LIMBO TANGO - OTHERWISE KNOWN AS THE FLAPPER FLOPPER ... 51
AFTER THE UMBILICAL VEIN WANES, THE BIRTH DEPT REMAINS ... 53
ILLUSIONS AND PERCEPTIONS ... 55
LITTLE BILLY DIY ... 57
IN SYNC ... 59
MISJUDGED MALEIA MEDITATING IN THE MEADOW ... 61
MINGLE LIMBO ... 63
MS. MAYZIE HAD A FLUFFY ... 65
NIGHT OF THE LIVING DEB ... 67
NITPICKERS ANONYMOUS ... 68
NOW ONLY NATURE KNOWS ... 71

MAGIC APPLES GROWN BY THE WRONG AUTHOR MUST BE IGNORED 73
QUESTIONABLE EXTRATERRESTRIALS 75
RAGE AND GLORY 77
SHIFTY GIFTING 79
PANTS ON FIRE 81
SADIE 83
OVER THE SHOULDER SCOLDERS OF THOSE WHO ARE BOLDER 85
SHE'S INVISIBLE NOW 87
TIME HAS A FUNNY WAY 89
COMMUNAL "YOU KNOWS" 91
SLEIGH-BOAT OF HOPE 93
THE DEAL OF THE DAY BECAME THE TALK OF THE TOWN 95
SARAMANE'S MUFFLED GRAVE 97
THE PROFIT FROM COLD WATERED TAILS 99
VOWEL-LADEN VERSIFIERS 101
ROAMING IN THE GLOAMING 103
WHAT DRIVES ME CRAZY? 105
WHICH WITCH'S WISH? 107
GULPINPLUMP 109
SOME BESTS ARE KEPT SECRET 111
BASEMENT RADICALS CRASHING MY SABBATICAL 113
SHEDDING TEARS WITH THE SHELLEYS 115
UNPREDICTABLE AUDIENCE 117
PATTY'S WAGON 119
UNIFACIAL RESPACEMENT 121
NO TASTO IN RELATIVE MINOR 123
ANATOMY APPROPRIATION 125
SKULLDROPS 127
ODE TO GENOLA 129
JUGULAR JONGLEUR 131
TWEET DEFEAT 133
SOCIAL FORUM POEM 135
LEECHES 137
THE IMPORTANCE OF POSITIVITY IS A PESSIMIST'S LAW DEGREE 138
BANZALTA DRAYN AND HER HATCHET-FAN PAIN 141
THE DEFEAT OF AMBERGIS 143
POSSESSED 145
ABOUT THE AUTHOR 147

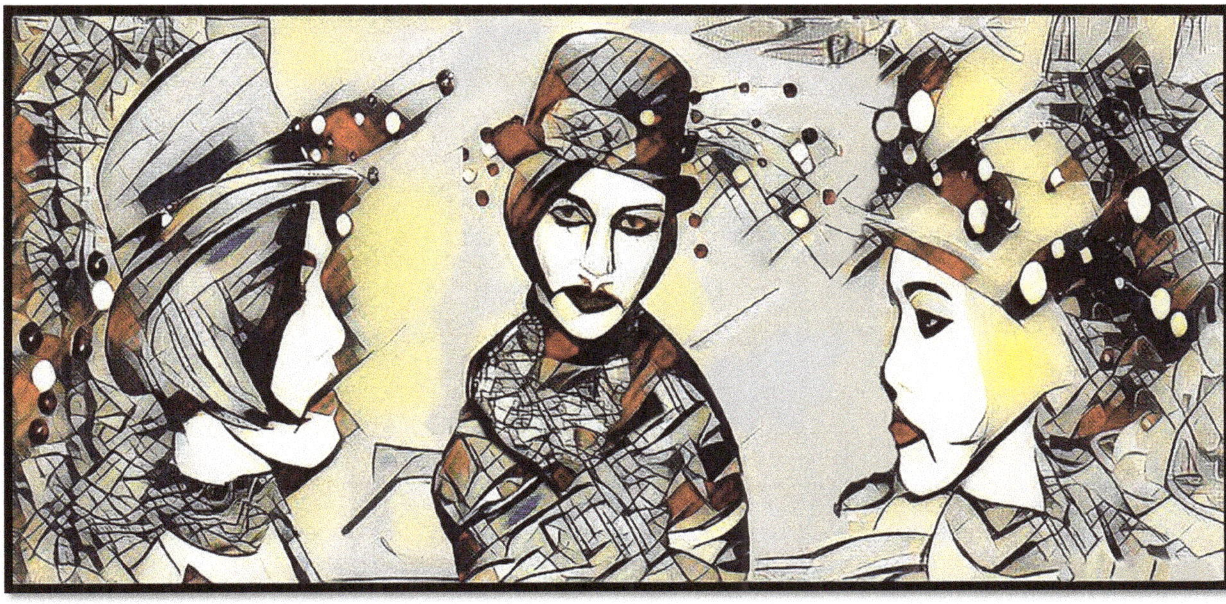

ATLAS OF CANDICE

The splash of the brush spoiled her milky pallor.
Moping about in frozen poses and autumn colors.
Twilight and morning, she's ignoring
The parameter of her canvas so boring.
Her hat a linear axis to such dashing abstractness.
Pivoting in the aftermath of painterly bliss,
All is sublime now; all is crimsonly crisp.

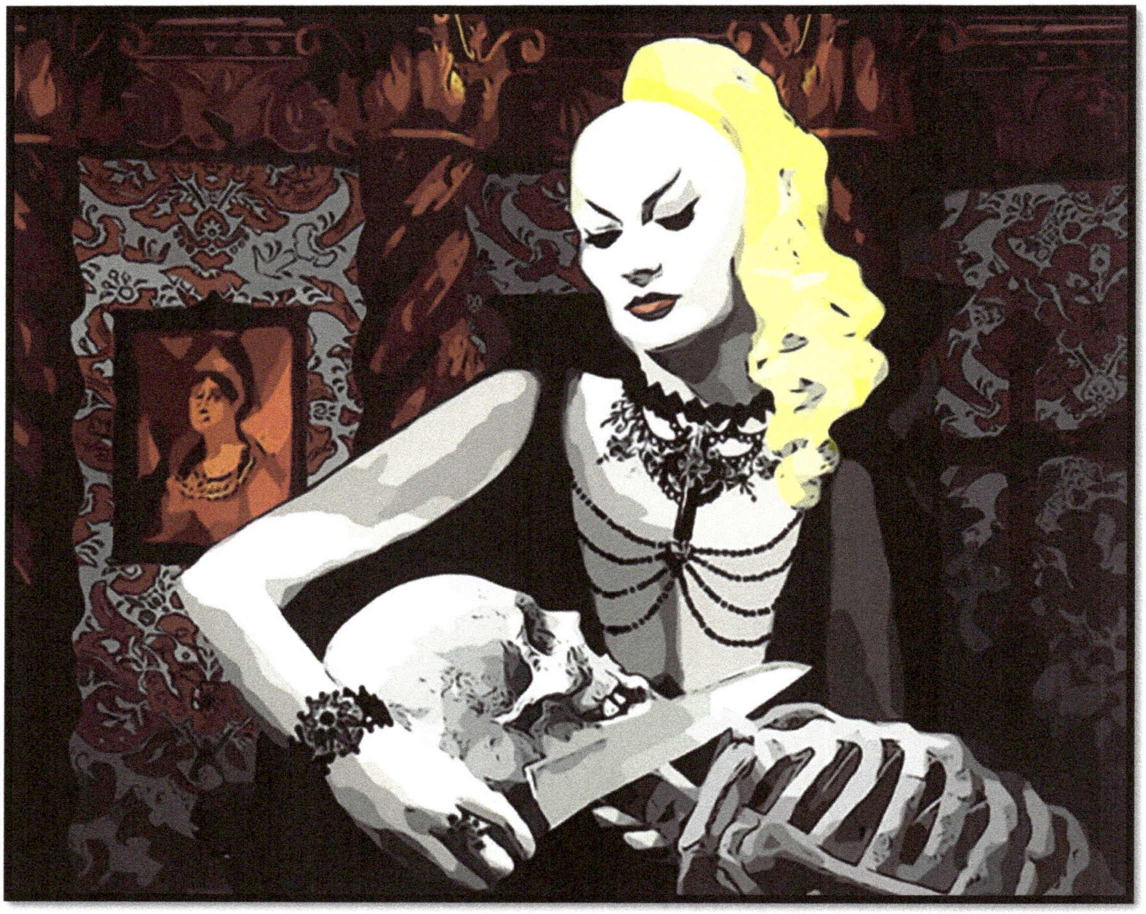

A REALLY CLOSE SHAVE

Weak days and nights long, feeble Roger Bethe would say,
"Renee, Renee, always you shave my face with a dud of a blade.
See! See this beard to my knees? Why, you've robbed me of my dignity."
This he would plead, 'til his jaws, they'd bleed,
And all his hair was gone by his dying day.

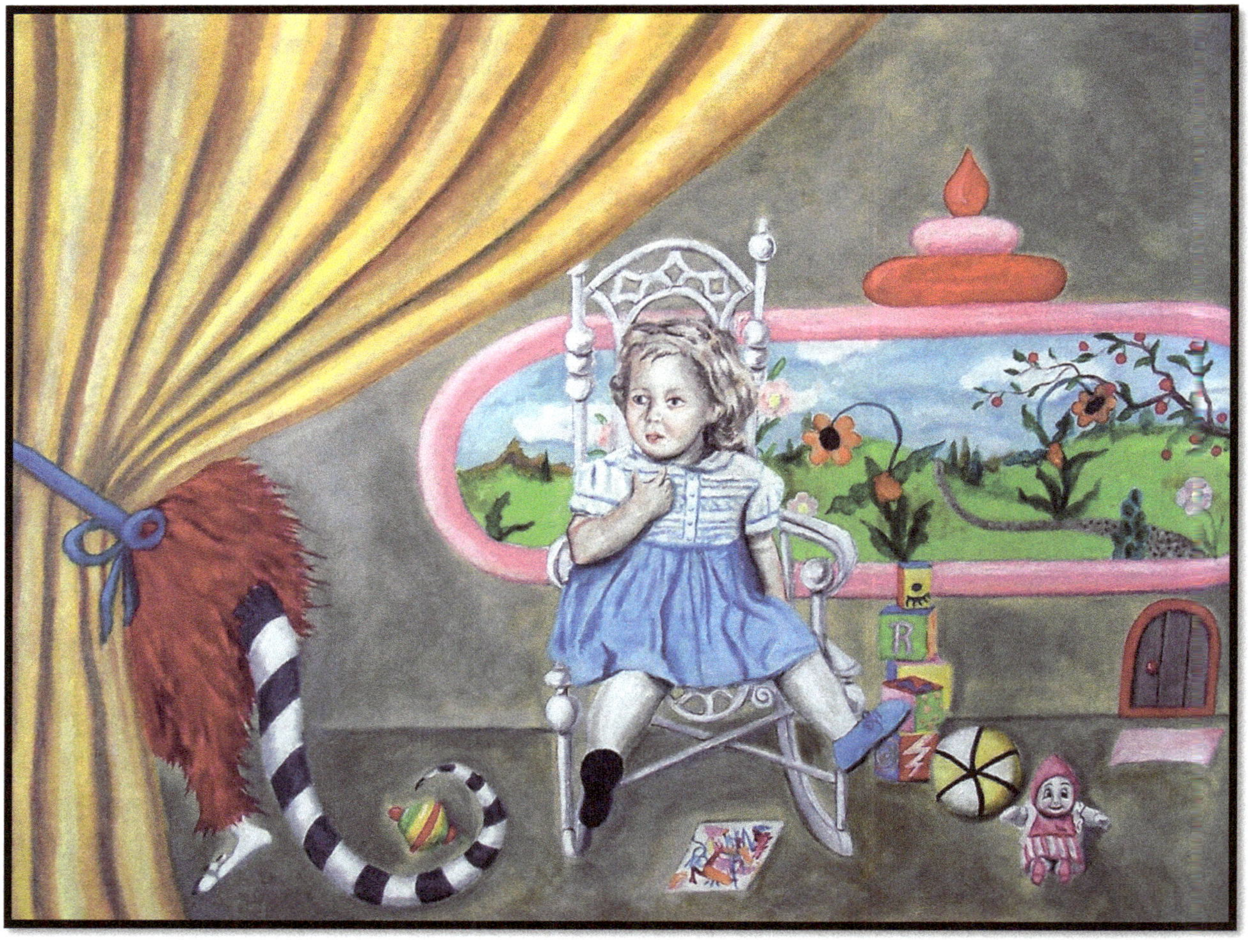

HOCKING UP THE CLOCK TONIGHT

Beautiful baby Becca brought her rocker to a stop
When her red rat stuffy ran off
With the cuckoo from her clock.
And as it lurked behind the curtain,
She couldn't quite determine
If her vermin, she called Herman,
Was speaking German
Or had a kooky cough.

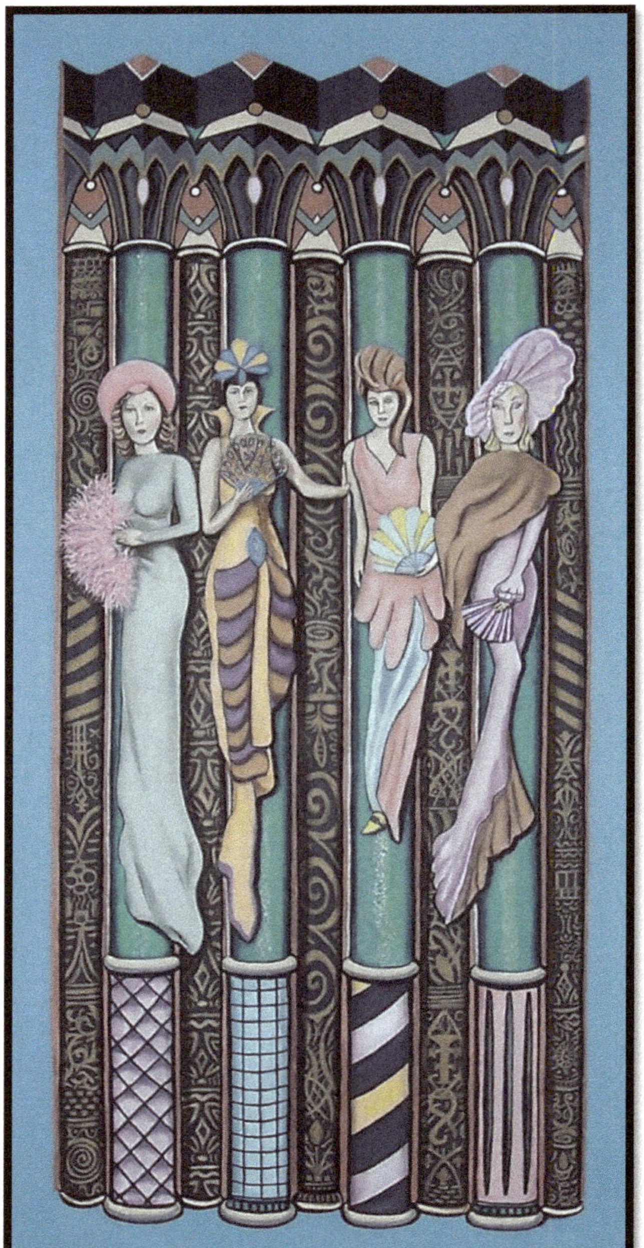

ADORING FANS

Four adoring fans
Unfolded in their hands
Fans of feathers, silk, and paper grand.
And on pedestals of aqua and sand
They struck a masterful stand,
Posing like plaster sirens
With strands
Of baubles to beat the band.

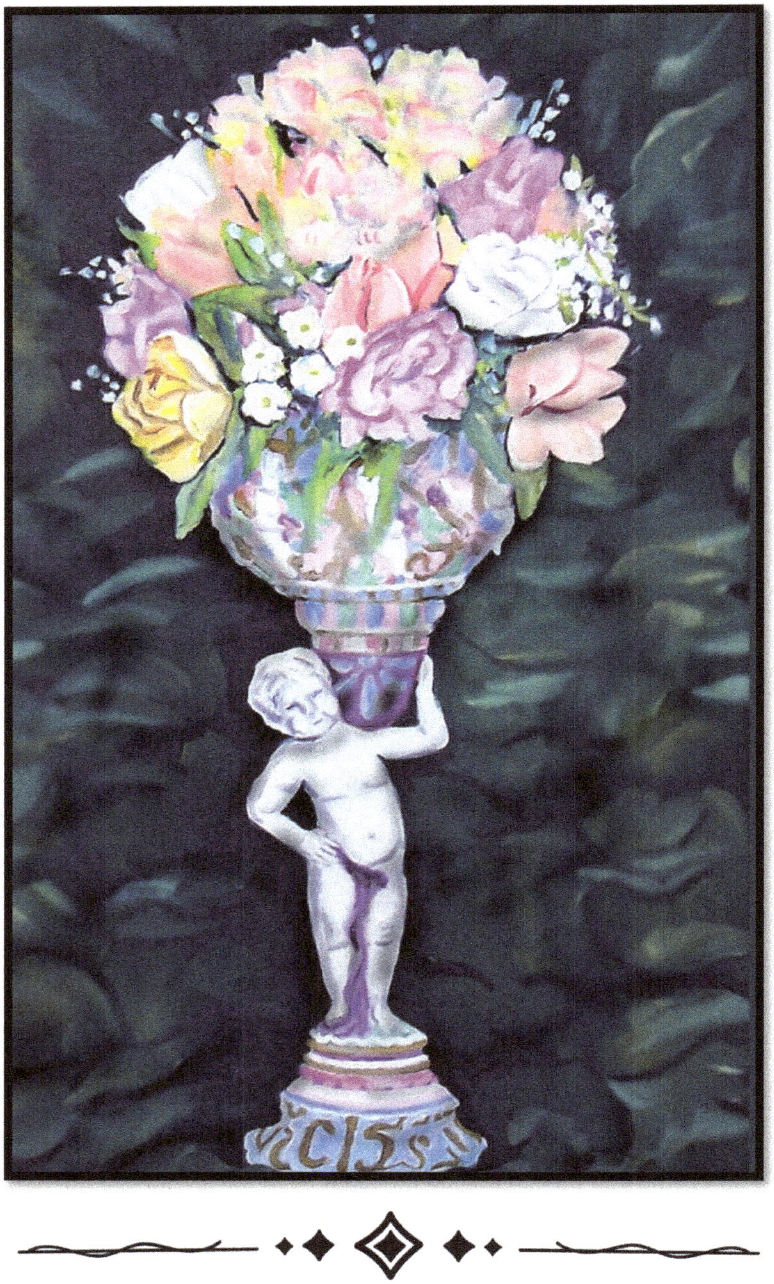

AGRICULTURAL ANGELOPHANY

Endlessly burdened by a bounty of budding beauty,
Alba Della bore the bouquet like a boulder
Upon his porcelain shoulder—
A fragrant spray against his crazed cheek,
Whilst his only sheath of modesty
Cascaded to his immobile feet.

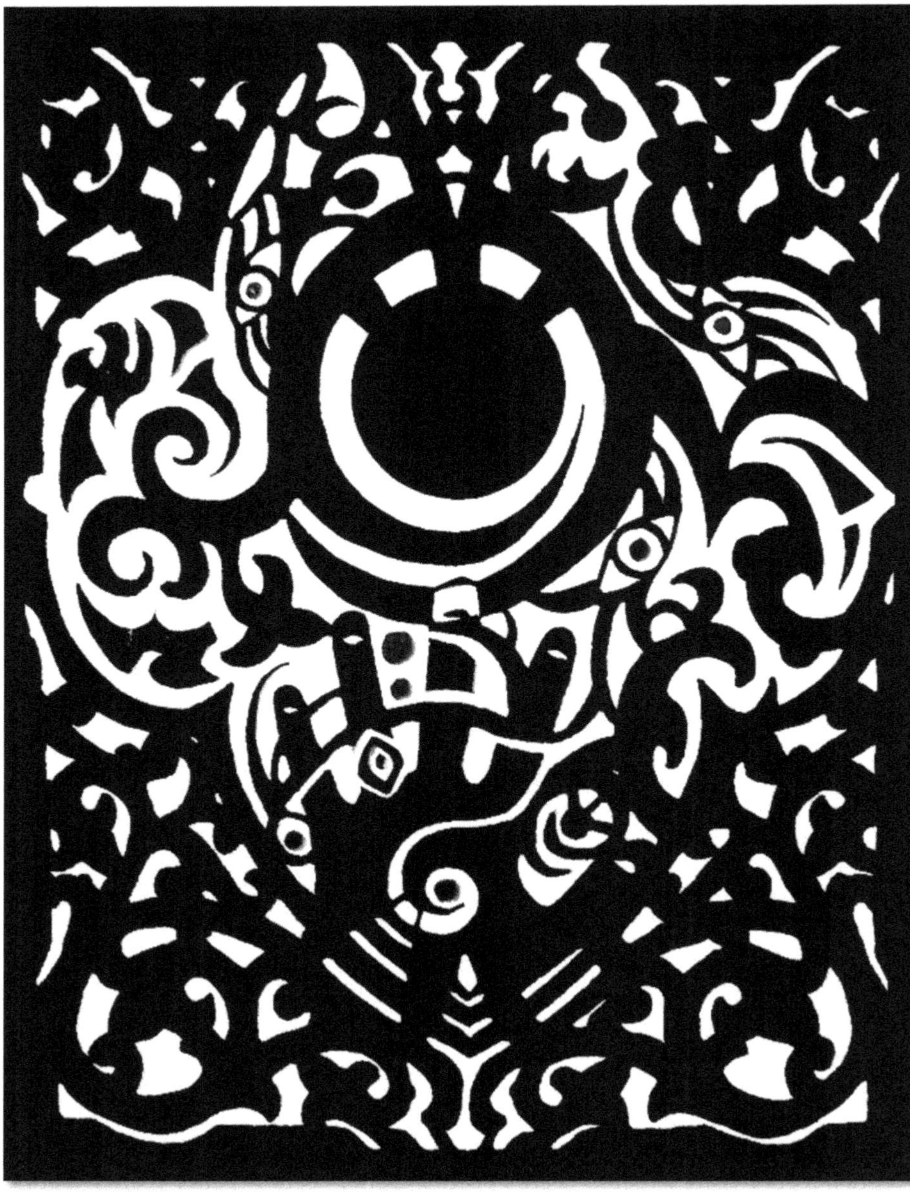

CIRCULAR CREDO

Peep through the window on the darkened street row
Under faded lamp glow.
Words on the sign show PRESTO TABLEAU.
So, with feelings of hope, you enter slow
To see Madame Bordeaux
Speak her mambo lingo in a voice deep and low.
"Give me all your dough for the end is in tow."
And for this you become broke,
Assuming she's in the know,
Some sort of sibylline hero.

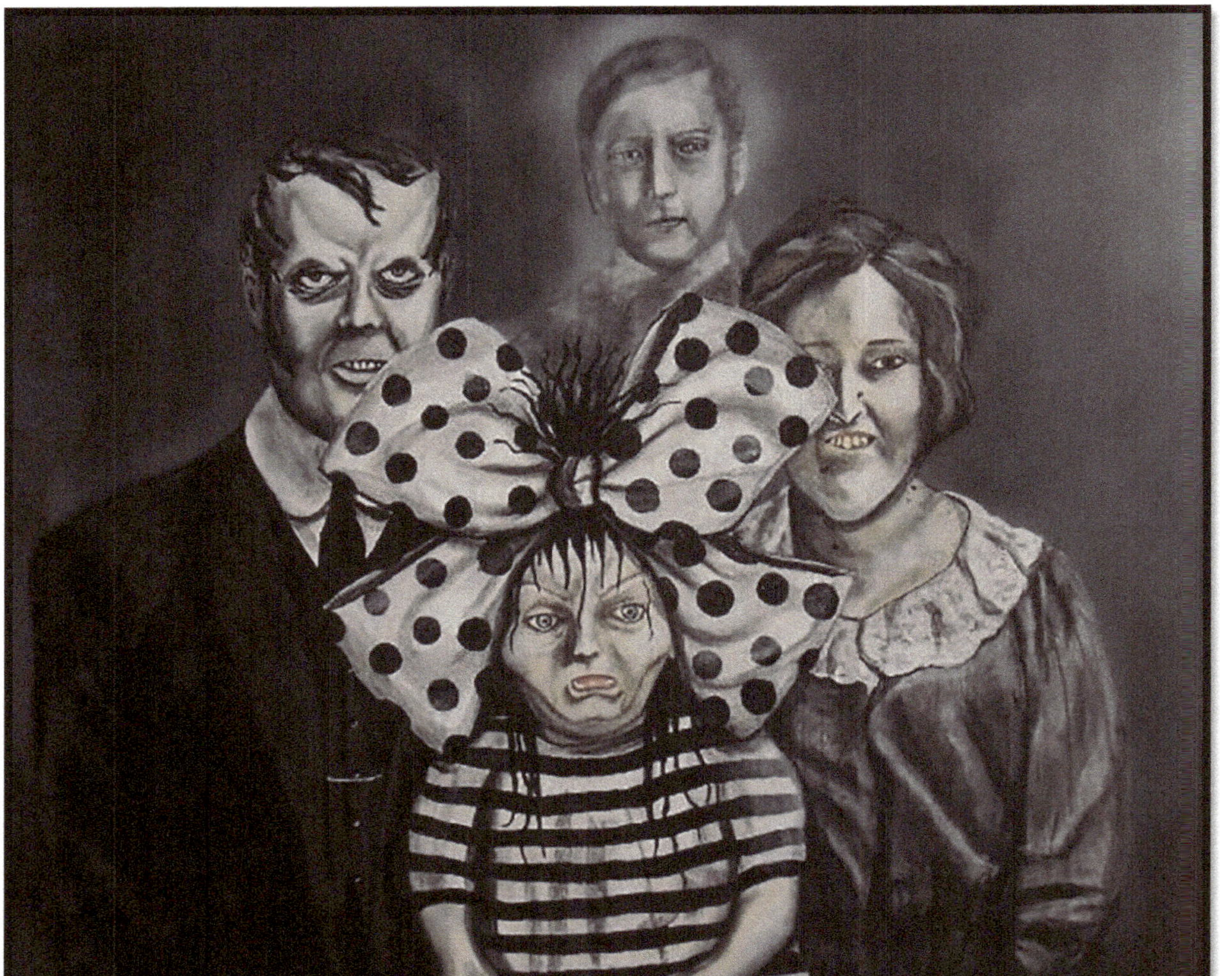

DEATH AMONG THE LIVING

I had an epiphany today:
With the wise things spirits should have to say,
Voices from the beyond always speak in clichés.
I couldn't wait to tell this to my nearest and dearest,
But it fell on deaf ears. What did I expect?
And then with pain, I realized
My creations and revelations — just the same — fell on blind eyes.
If things couldn't get any bleaker — my whole life became a cruel mirror,
With me over here and the world nowhere nearer.
Yes, I teared. I brooded 'til I was sore.
There's no time in this world for certain realists — they're awful bores.
I cracked jokes — became a clown marionette,
Got laughs for a moment — a weekend bandage at best.
So, I wrote in the fantasy — living there's more soothing.
Many sneaked peeks at me, but the change was unmoving.
Now, here lies the irony:
In spotlighted lives — pretend is for movies.
And so, it was then — my destiny and past started to blend.
For I really must comprehend,
My mind is for apparitions — residual repetitions,
And I — am my only friend.

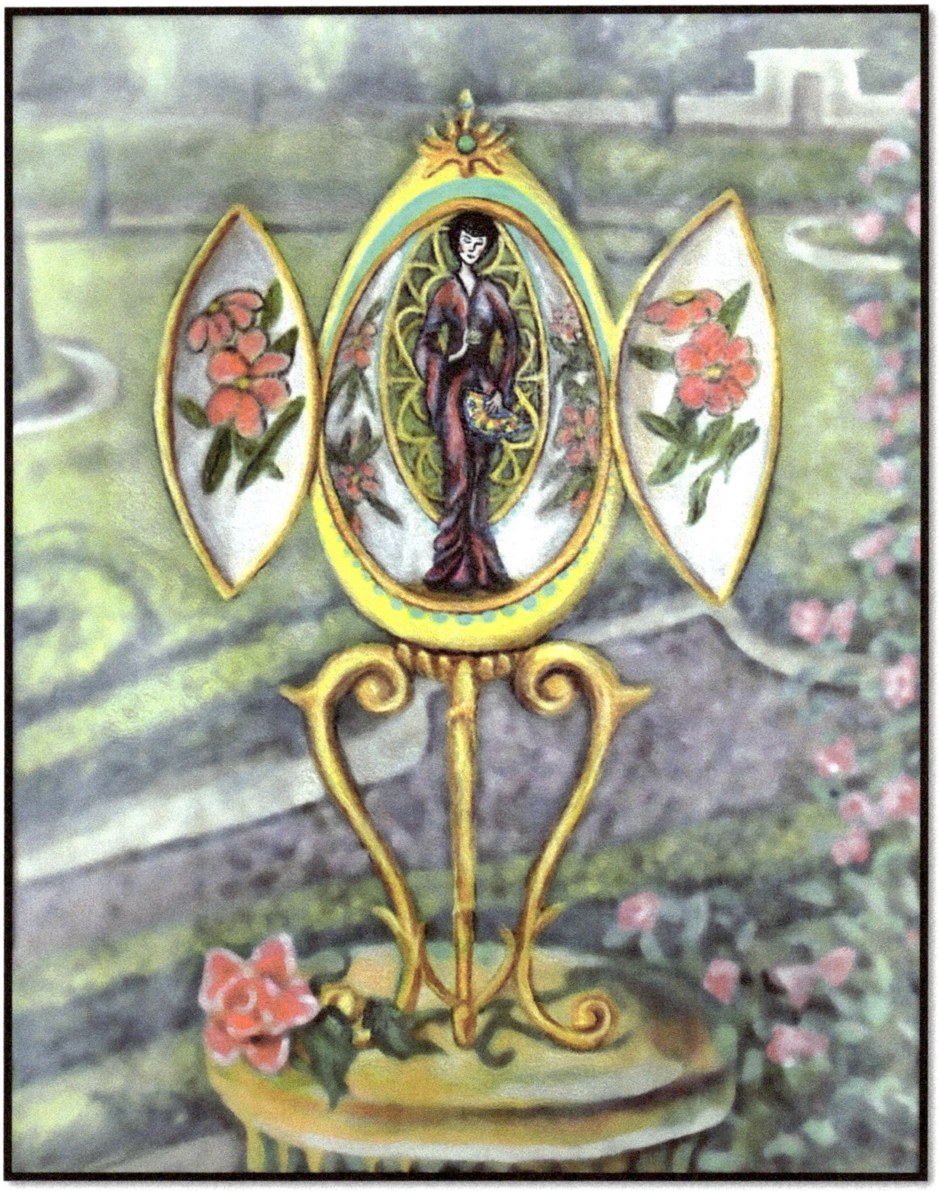

EMERGE

Su Chi hatches from her egg laid golden,
O'er the goose-feathered garden from Mother's molting.
In the cool winter sun, she's quite a vision,
Whispering songs of hope and words of wisdom.
"Children of Earth, you must take heed.
You are one with nature. You are Mother, indeed.
Cherish the planet and don't forsake her.
Your skin is grass, your hair, its leaves.
These become cancers and worldly disasters
With all the heartless trash you heap,
Thinking you and yours will live for now,
And for the next generation, you'll leave
All your refuse to stumble o'er and clean."

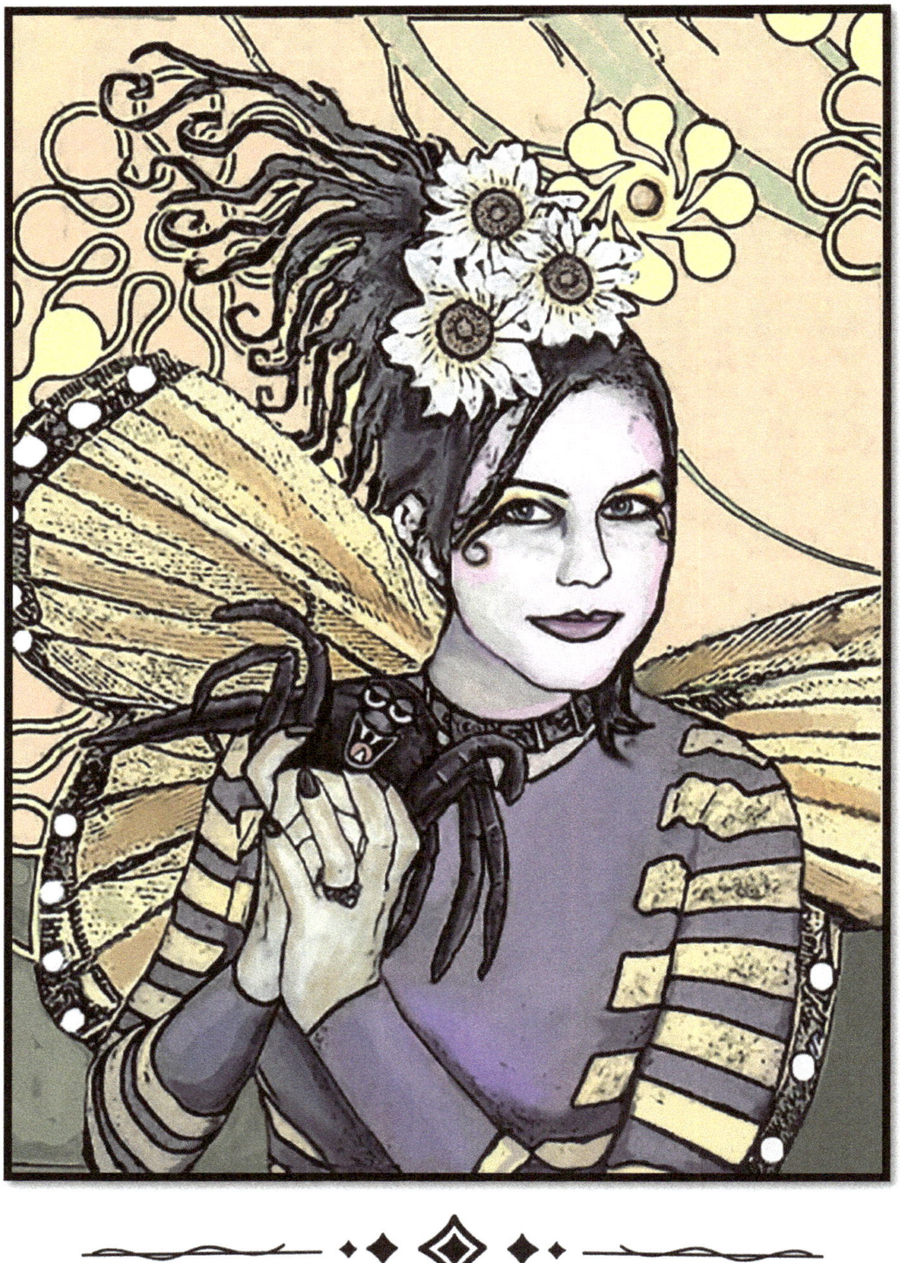

FAIRIES

Far from the camellias of the blessed,
Where blossoms sway betwixt leaves laden with lazy steam,
Dewey-skinned fairies drift like seedpods,
Carrying spiders —
Venomous orchids —
Against their chests.

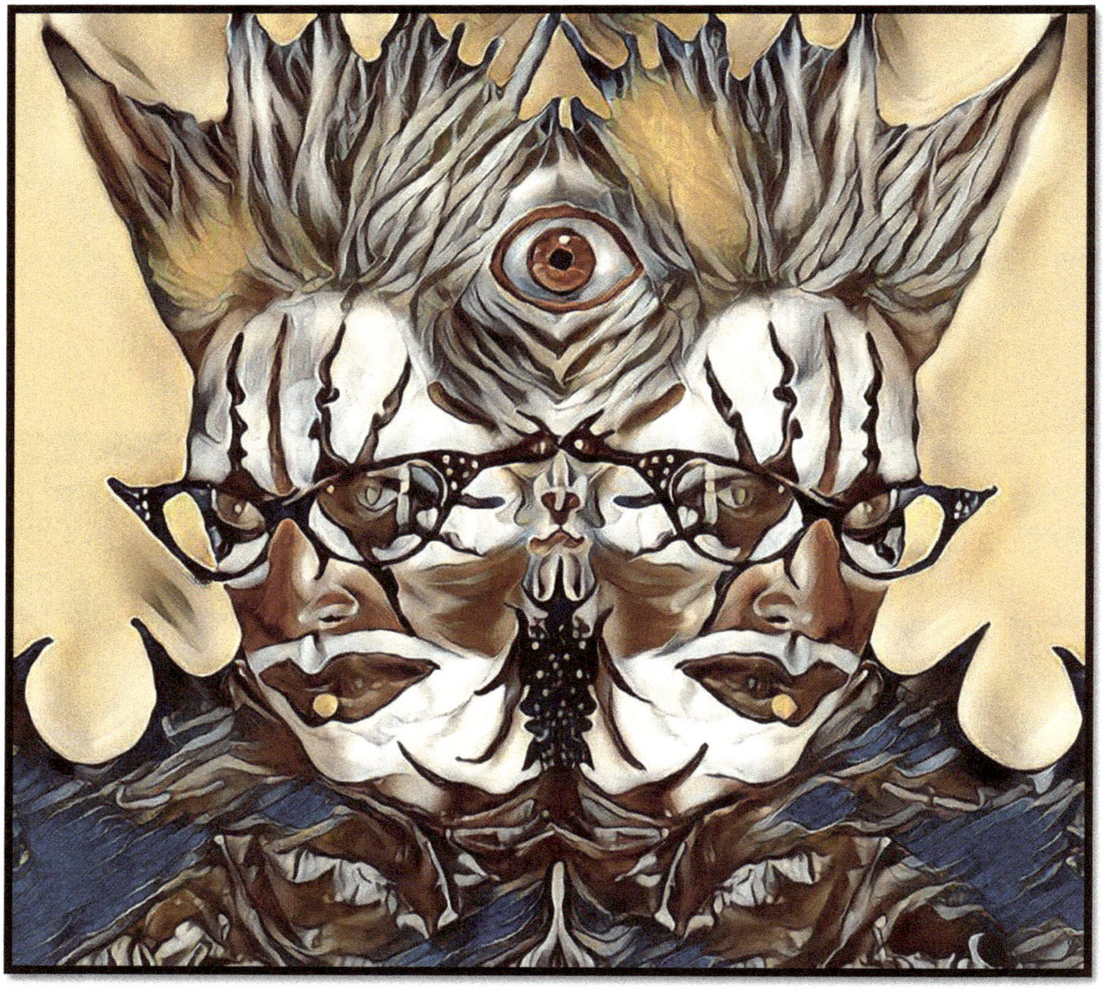

I.C.U.

Incorrigible Connie never found her style funny.
Her hair was pristine and makeup, subtle.
No demon she dared not face
'Til she started seeing double.

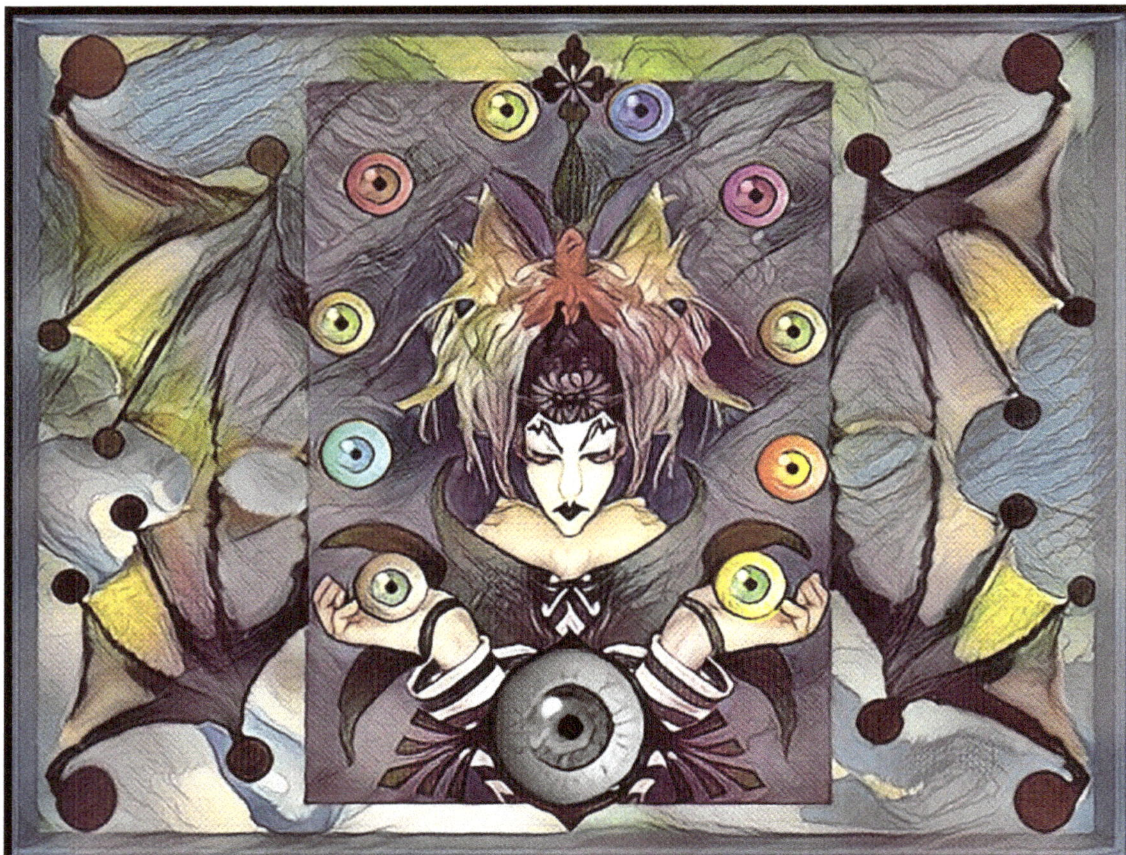

FALLUCINATIONS

Do not hear the sounds I shall shout at the ground
O'er your outta-bounds exit.
Oops! Your academic ear doubted my cacophonous psyche.
You fear you'll be flouted.
'Twas no truer lie touted.
Now, see my frown on fabricated monuments
As you become a mage in circular tournaments —
Pages à la hogwash firmament.
Engage pain and a low lot, knowing your plight is a faux pas
And my name was alas conjured in vain.

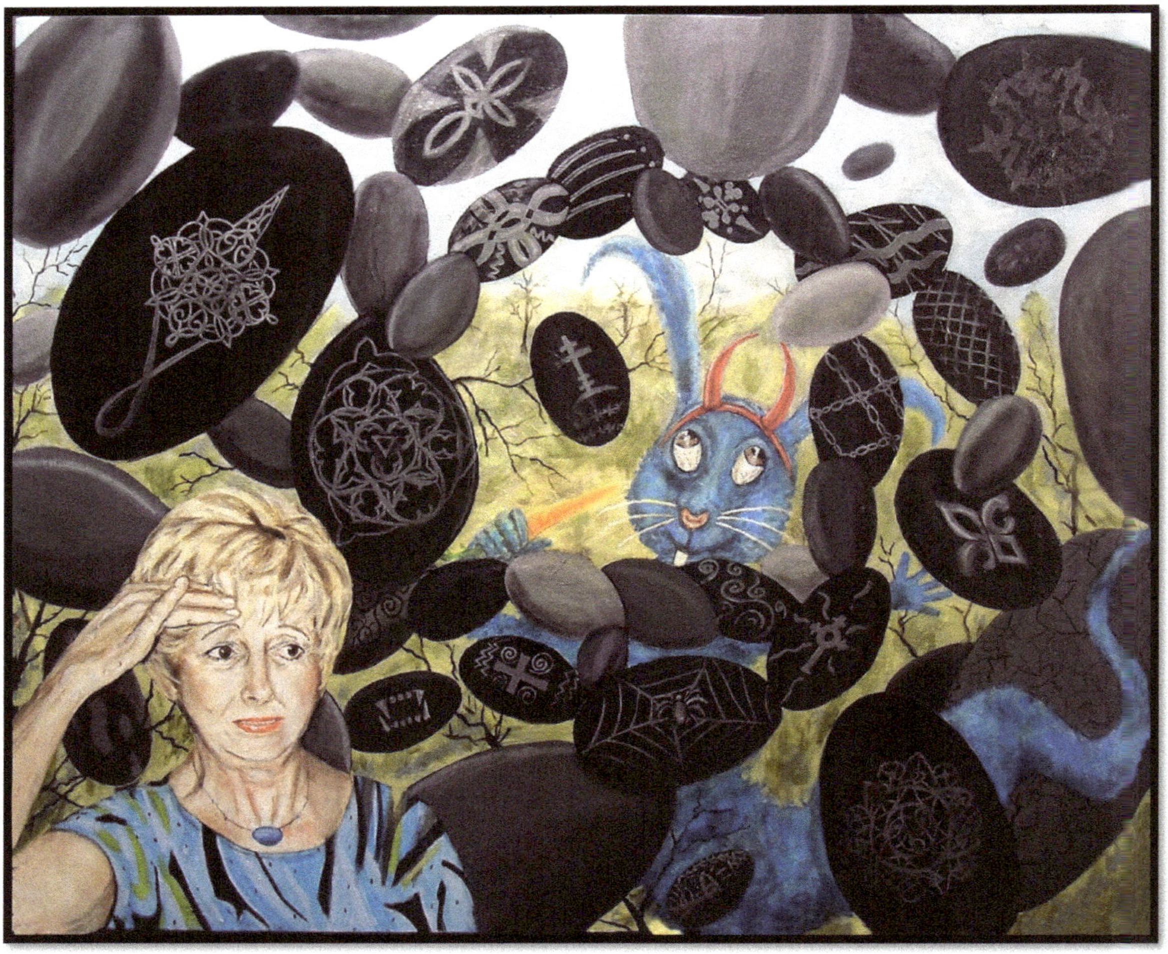

SOME TALES ARE FLUFFIER THAN OTHERS

Oh dear! Who dyed the Easter eggs black?
I fear my little noggin will crack!
Ew! The Easter Bunny's not blue.
And what's with his bonnet?
Is that the Roman numeral two?

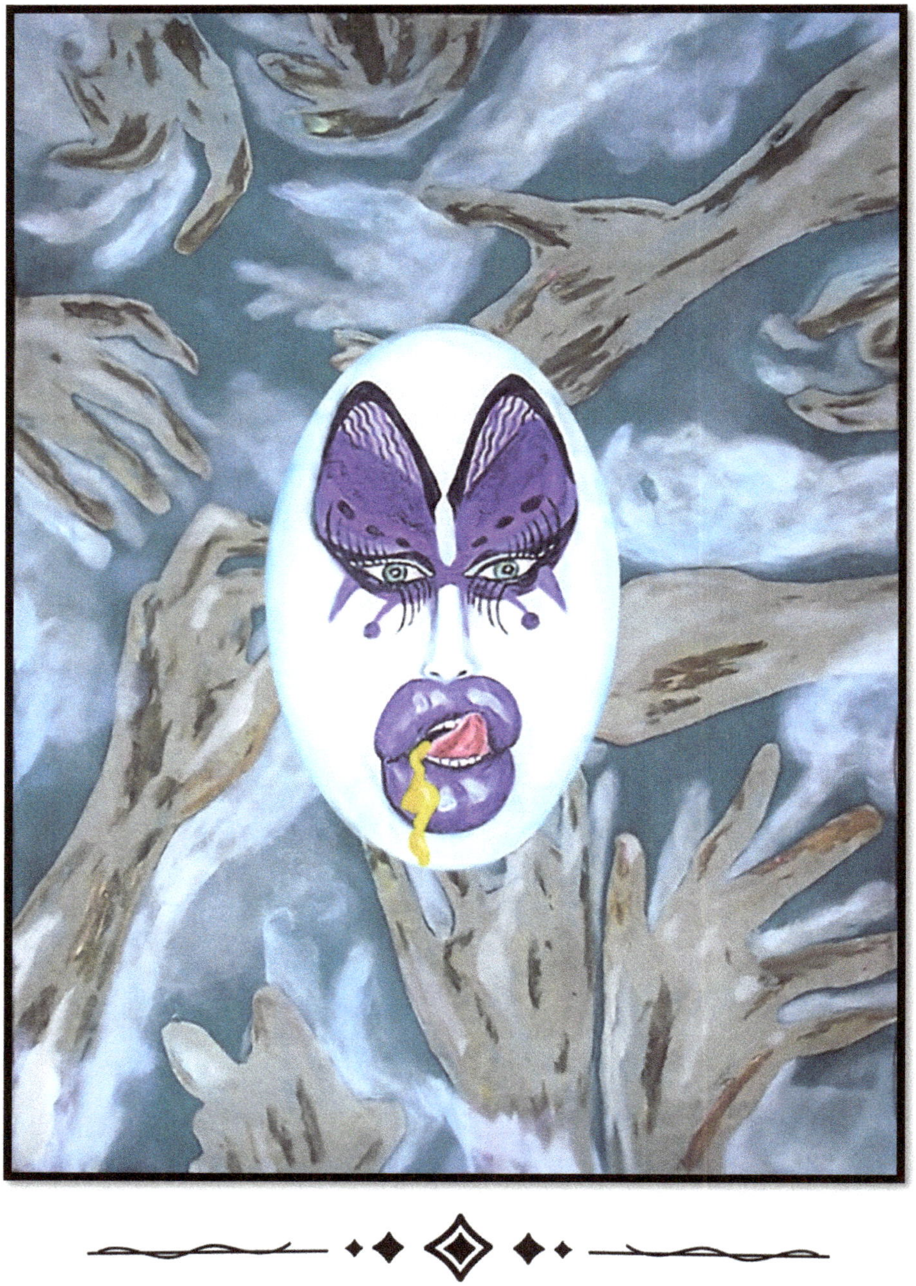

CHEAPER BY THE DOZEN - THE UNYOKING OF THE GOLDEN EGG

I'm not here to be another egg in your basket of rottens,
Plucked on a whim, dyed, and then forgotten,
Or to be poached, scrambled, or flipped
Under the spatula in your vandalous fist.
I'm an egg meant to hatch, to grow and spread my wings,
And do as I wish.

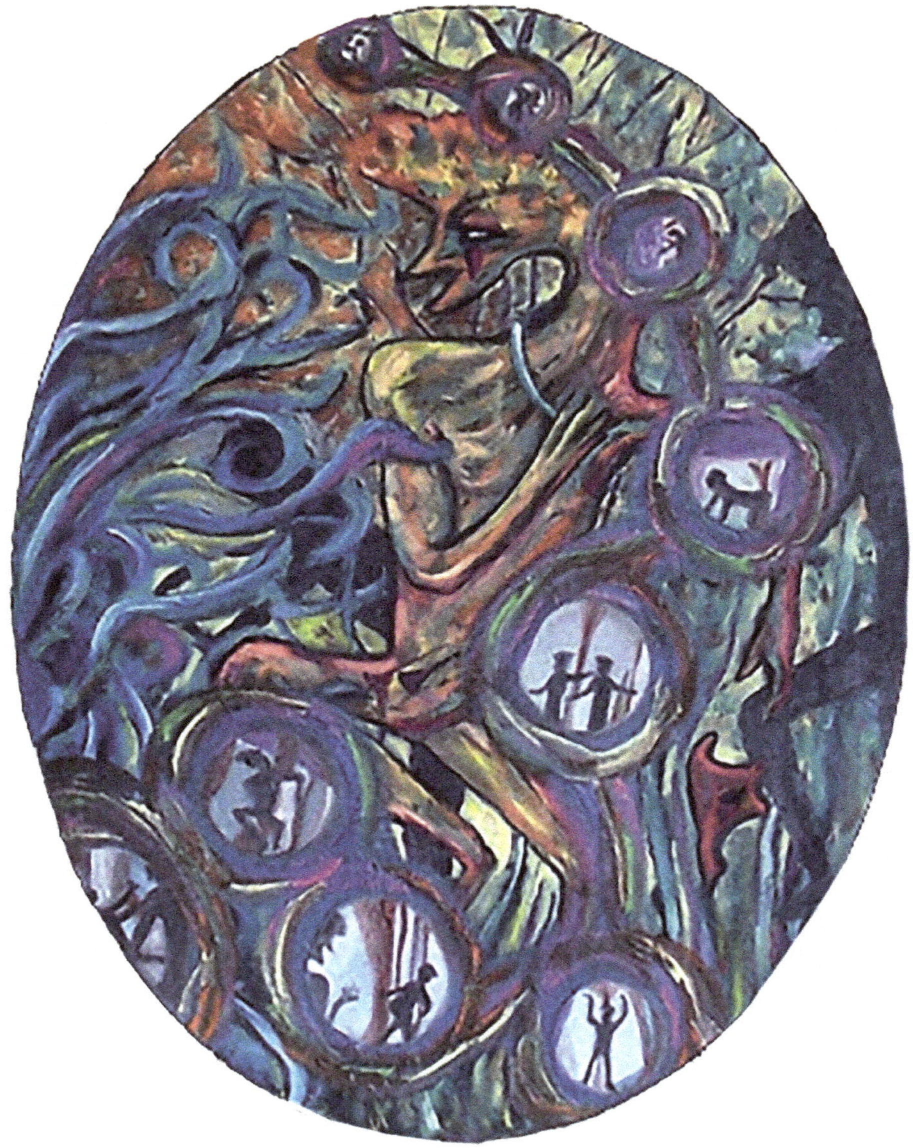

FATE'S FICKLE FINGER

As Fortune's uncertain path waxed and waned,
He awaits Fate's eternal scrolls to penetrate the vast vortex
And decide his place.
Dumbfounded and screaming inside at the pernicious
Root of gossip spreading,
Eyes prying, and bets placing, Fortune became misplaced
When Fate callously closed the gates on his pace.
"O Fortune, fret not; for the eating lichen feast upon the unworthy,
While the wings of the Blessed flutter in their secure nests
Collecting debts and saving face."

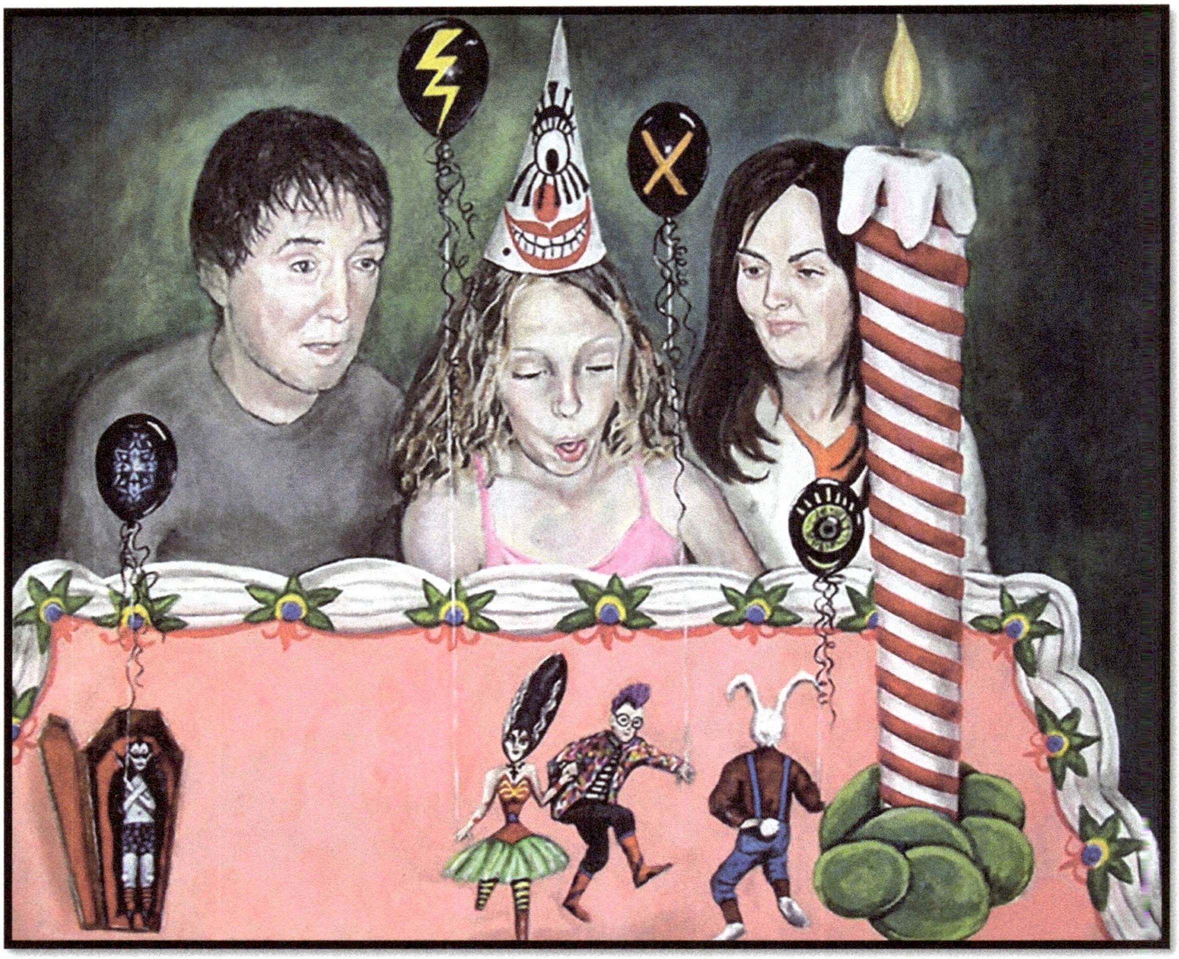

FROSTED PHENOMENON

The power is up for grabs
When you make a wish and wear a hat.
So, blow out the candles on this your birthday,
And hope that you can handle
The fruition of the wish you made.

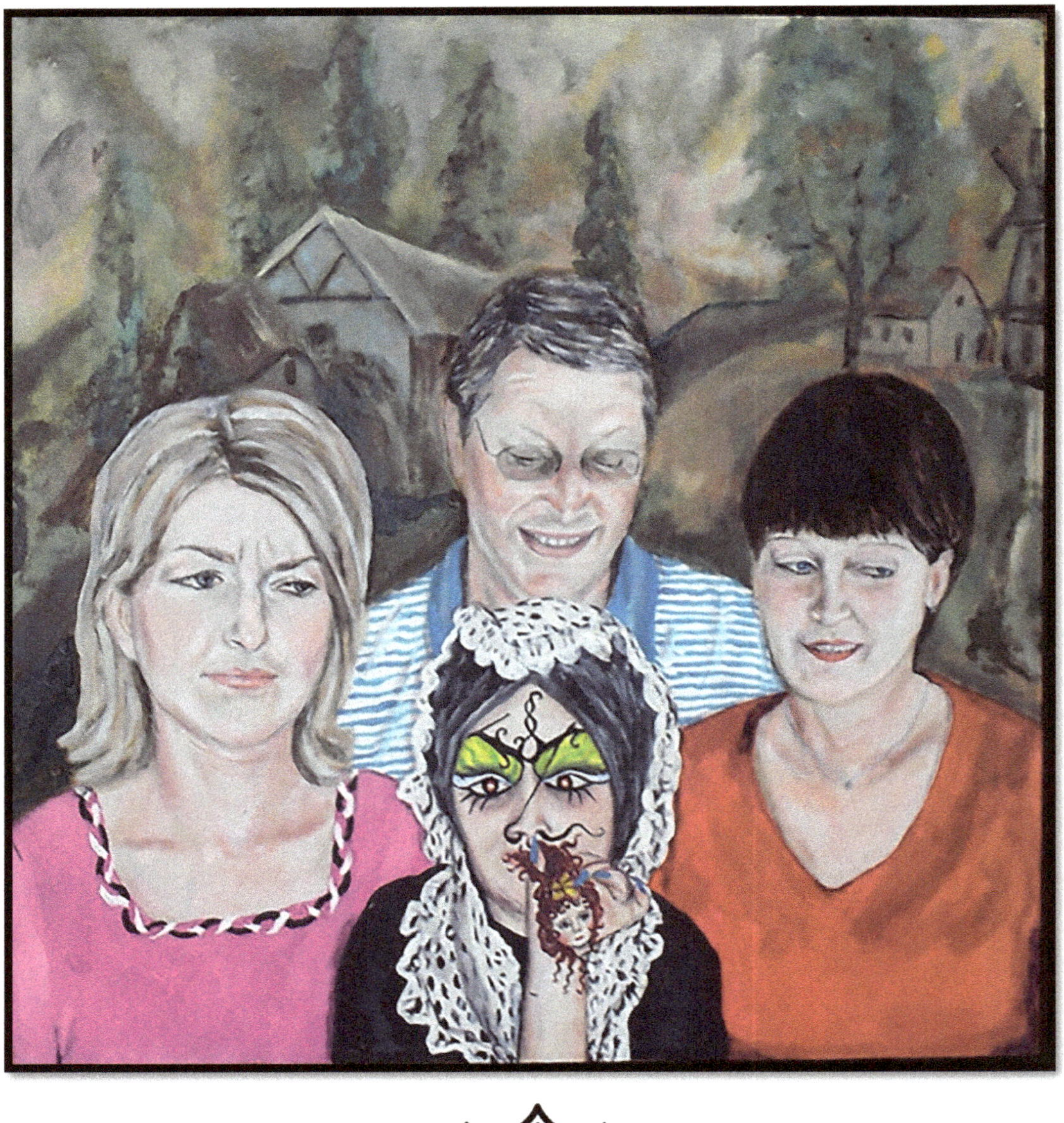

DEADHEAD THE DANDELIONS

Pansy's perennial intermingle at the reunion
Was like a stink-flower blooming amid camera lenses zooming
On the purest pedigrees pruning renegade weeds intruding.
And with disdain brewing, there was a lot of assuming
That it was a deadhead retribution Pansy was chewing,
But she's merely pursuing uprooting to a garden of union.

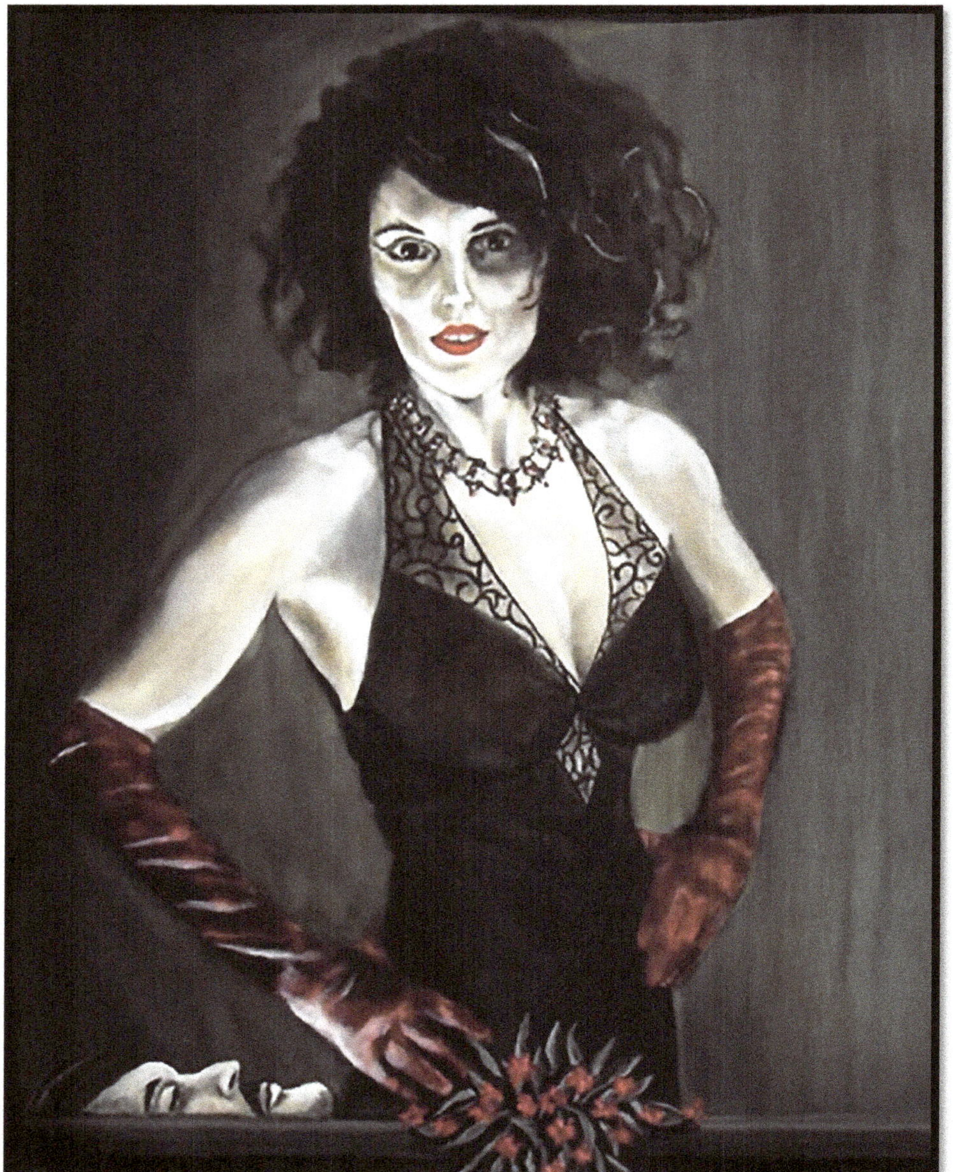

UNDERNEATH MODEST DAYWEAR IS THE EVENING'S LEATHER AND DARE

Pretend this is a series you watch every evening.
I know you do.
Don't compartmentalize your feelings
Now that you see death in a different media.
This is Edith, but her heart's not bleeding
For Norm, you see.
"Sometimes the groom's flower withers fast
On the lapel it adorns."
For even the cosmos itself avails to ignore
The misfortune of some,
Leaving Edith's victims defenseless in my world of moans.
No, here Norm shall remain adrift
On the River Styx forevermore
Alone.

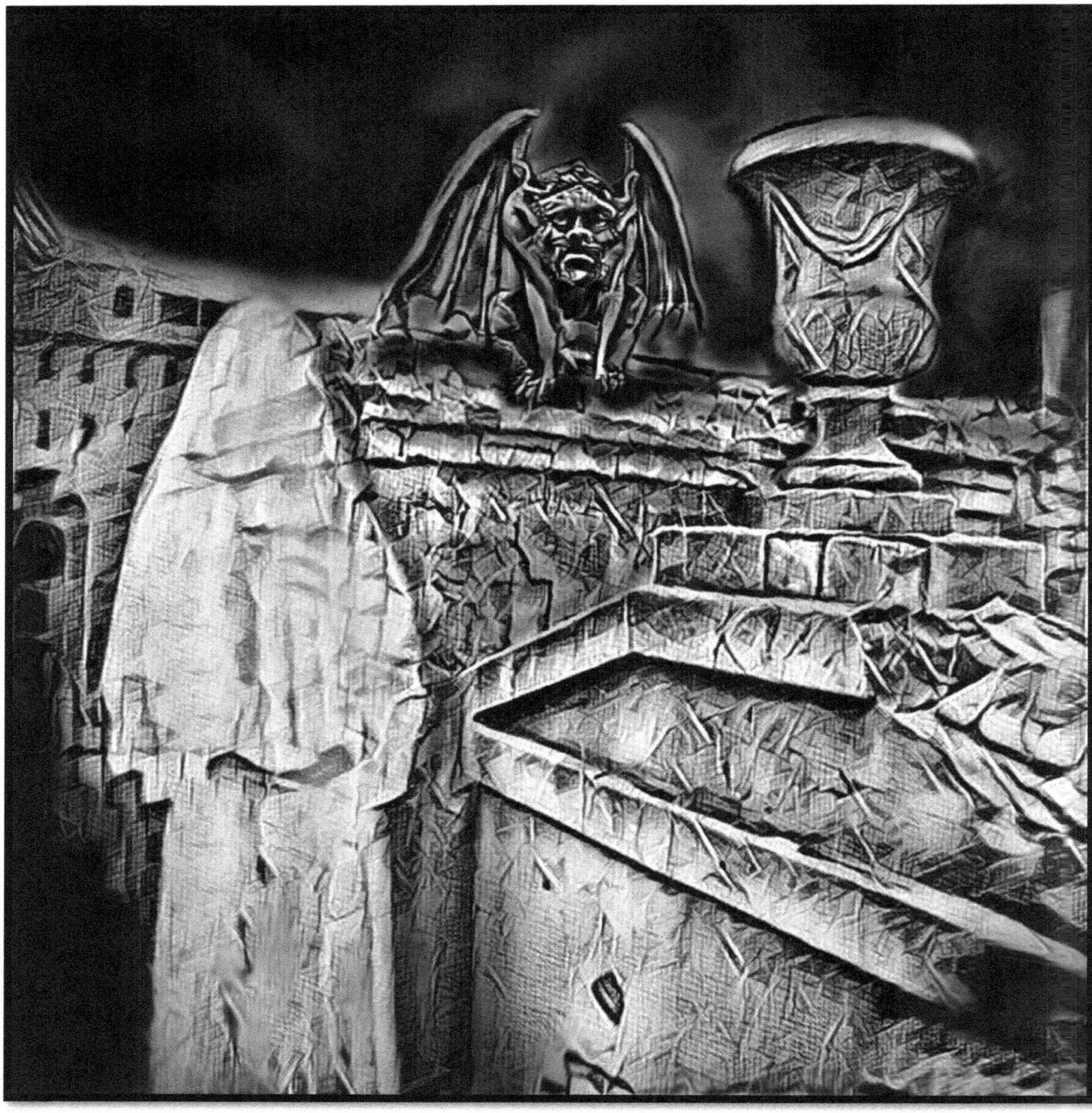

ONLY DEATH SURVIVES

Feast your eyes on the disenchanted souls,
Perched high, with black wings unfurled,
On the death chambers lone,
Phantom-weary from flapping death's bones,
Listening to the dull tones of passing chimes
As waves of bitterness compel the shores of time
To lend forth secrets.
Return them not into the grasping hands
Of the Reaper.

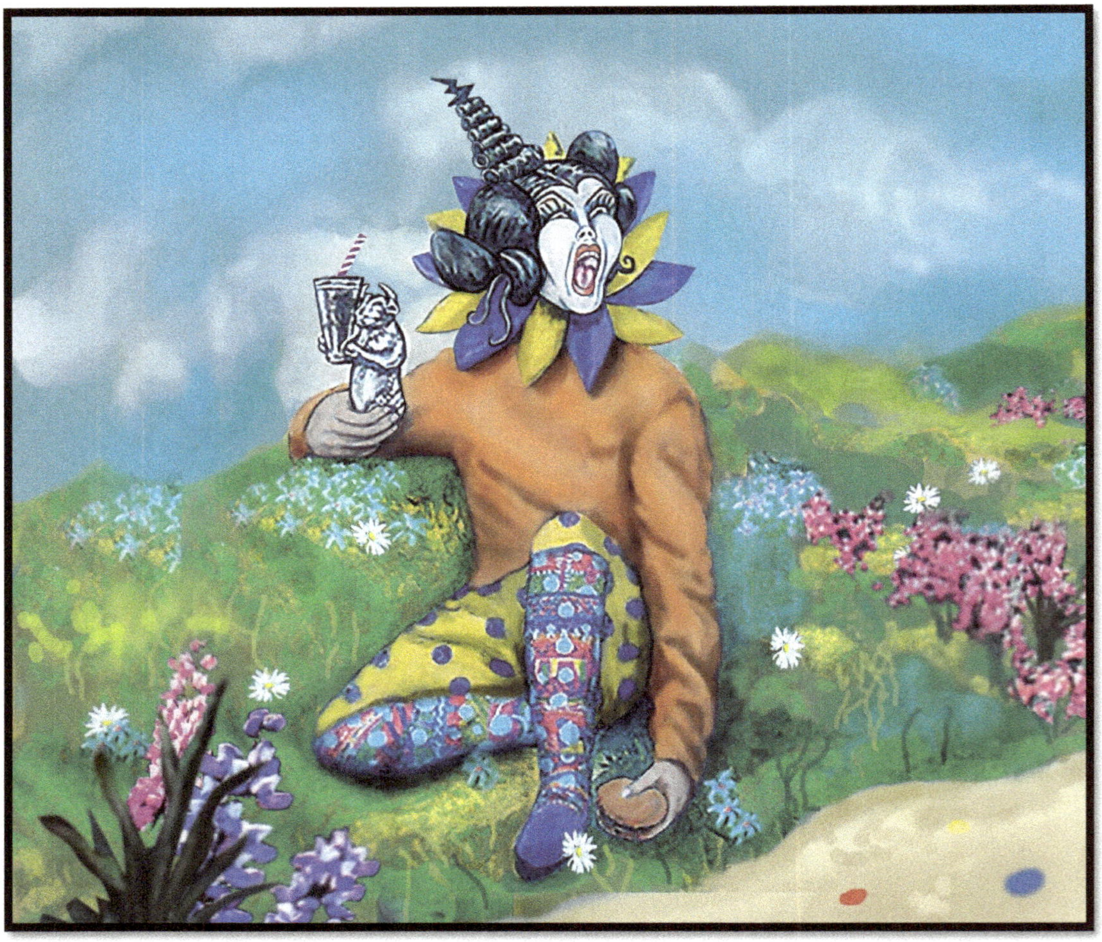

FUSIHATCHI'S OOKY DAY

Lounging in the rolling glen
Sipping Sacred Cow-Aid,
Fusihatchi contemplated
The pickly sandwich her momma made.
Then she belted out a boomer,
When a bee flew up her bloomers,
And she was fifty minutes late
For the parade.

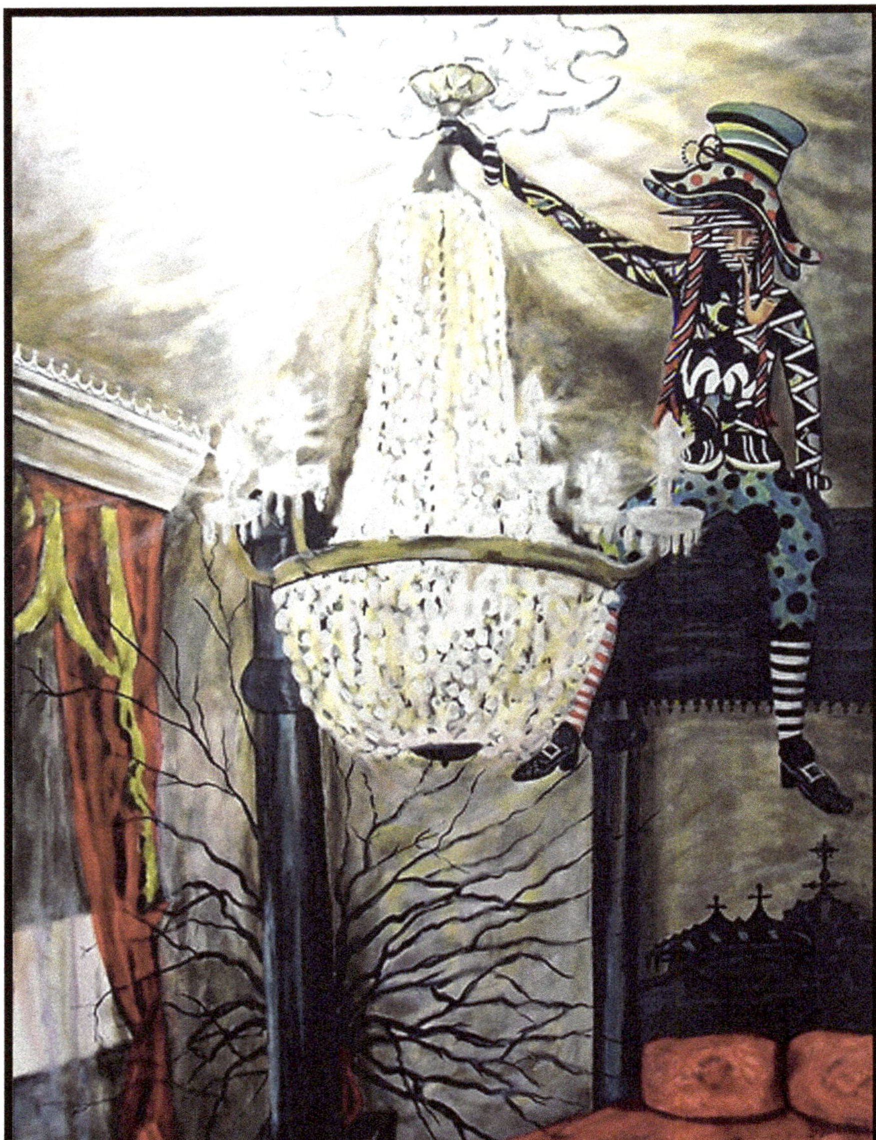

GO TO THE LIGHT

Old Rasta Dickens went to the light in his
Stove-pipe hat and ragamuffin britches.
But dread locked his Buffalo gal
In loving apprehension
When she saw, with affright, his apparition
Floating in the kitchen
While puffing on a pipe.

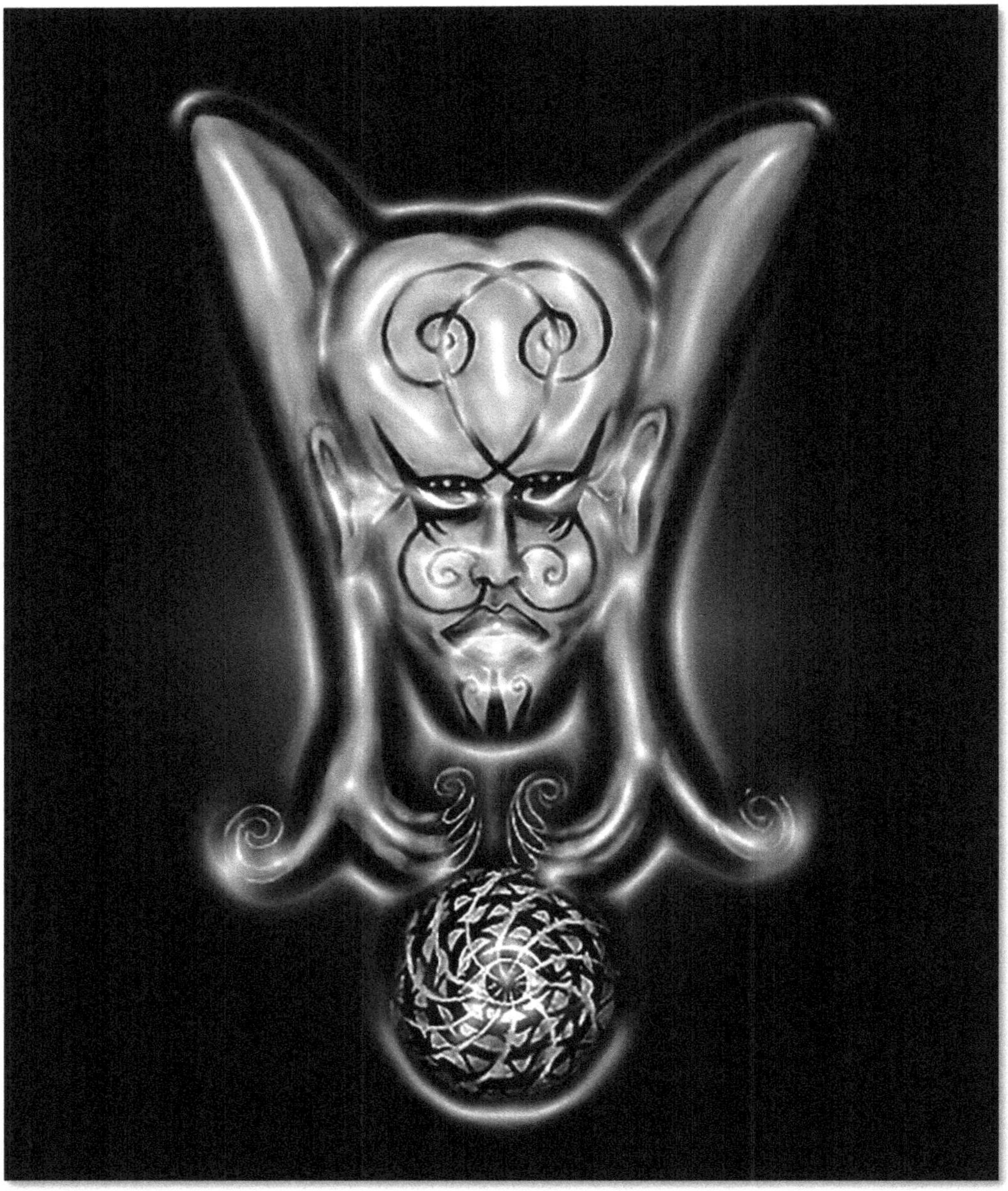

MORTAL MORSEL'S DOMINION

Even my dying breath you shall breathe —
The longing encrypted on a former heart's reed.
Your mission releases as you foresee:
'Twas deeper than opinion, our mortal morsel's dominion.
Shoegazing coven with earnest, hazy craving
Gloominous bequest past Eden's demanding.
Part of the belly —
So many cords.
Plexus knots expanding —
All from some words.
Tearstains, dried on the new command altar, now fire
The guns of subliminal slaughter.
This muteness on me you brought so young may return
And repair this yare you call care.
Tho' it renders tenebrific, to which I question the unspecific
You shall no doubt cherish the breaking of my tongue.

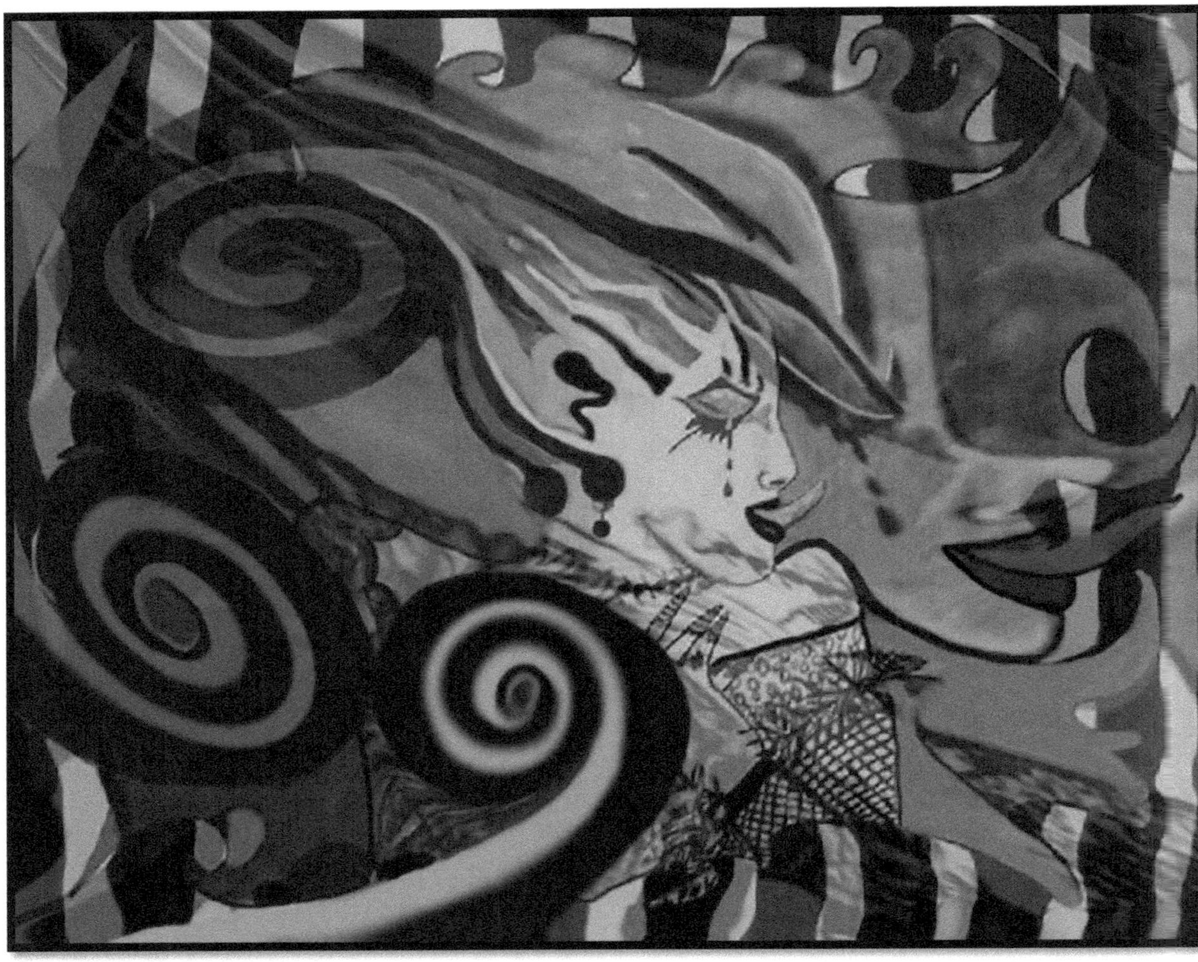

LOLLIES

Lyla loved lollies,
Churning, swirling lollies.
She could taste them in the air.
And for sticky, sculptured dare,
She would wear them in her hair.
A superb sugar scrub in her bath
To glaze her skin like bubble glass,
Her purple-scented body.

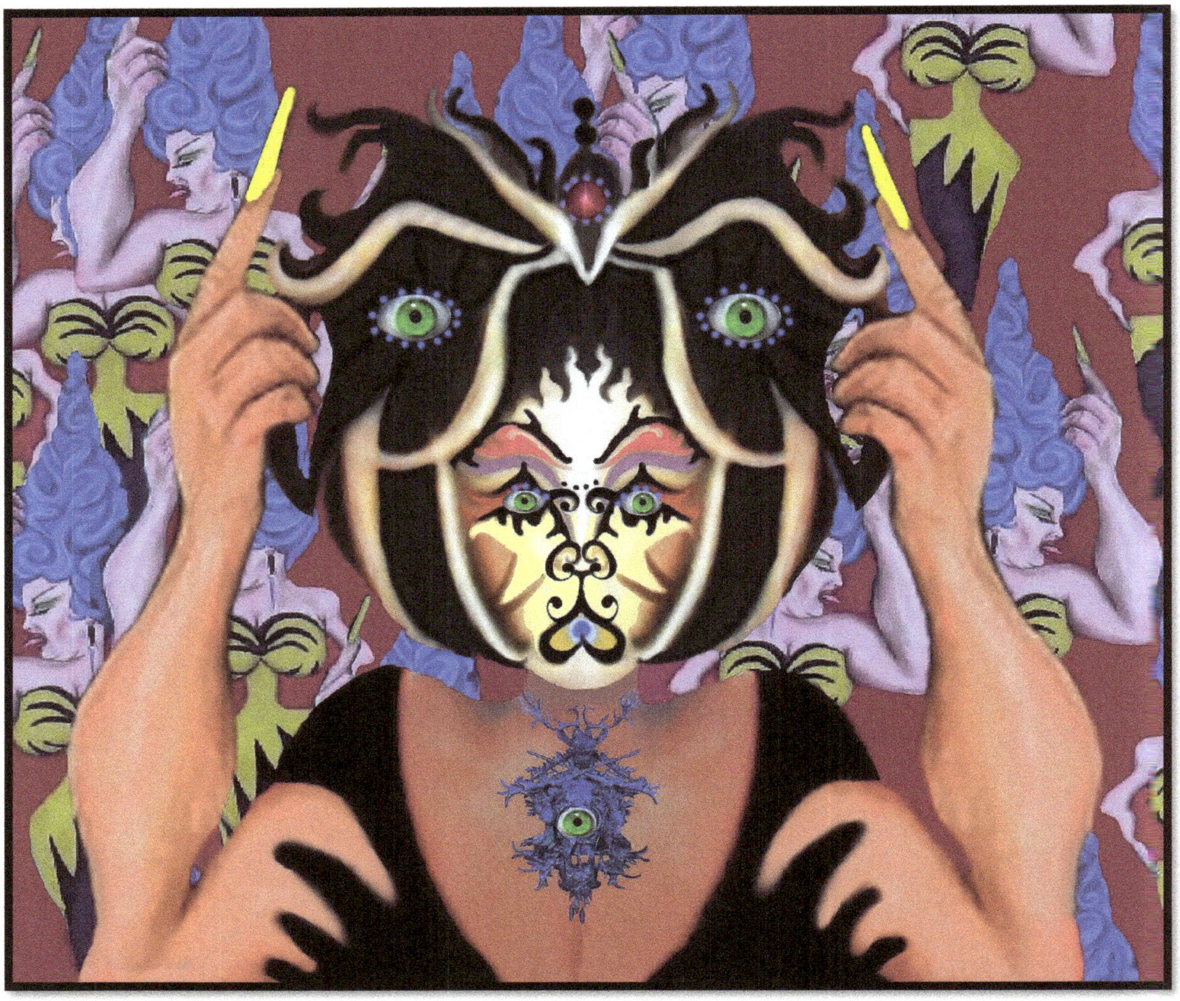

MADAME DACTYLIC

I'm just a springboard for her evening peeks.
Trigger-happy eyelashes flapping —
Another target she seeks.
Craving madness in her brain, ostracizing when it came.
Playing silence like a card. Intimate consummates
Vacillation from afar.
Wielding scissors for the slice — 'tis her nest-bound
Wingless flight.
Manipulated mystery. Screen from rain.
Solo chess games in the pain.
Dada tactics made her Madame Dactylic.
Nada rebirth. Instant tactic.
Opportunity's prophylactic.

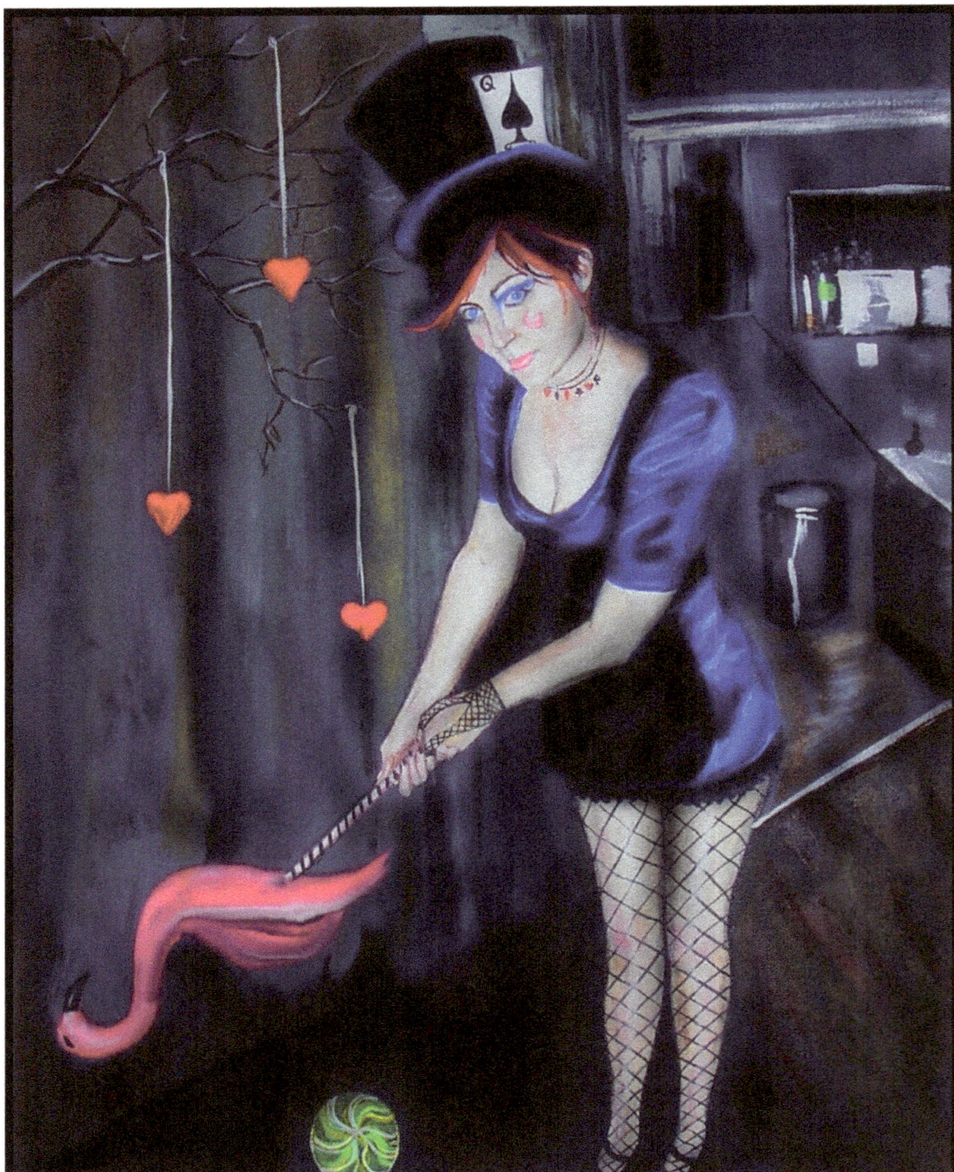

HEARTS ON STRINGS

Listen to the chimes of eternity.
Hear their beckoning.
No man holds the epithet of her fate.
She is immortal, not a ghost without reflection.
Hence, her body shall dwell evermore in Memorial Park.
Her pale skin sublimely blanched.
She can no more nobly repress the pangs of
Her enraptured poisoning,
Though regret turns on its foot — evermore.
Until never's end, revisiting fond old memories,
Where melancholy clovers sway in
Fields of human recollection,
And hearts on strings yield no disappointment.

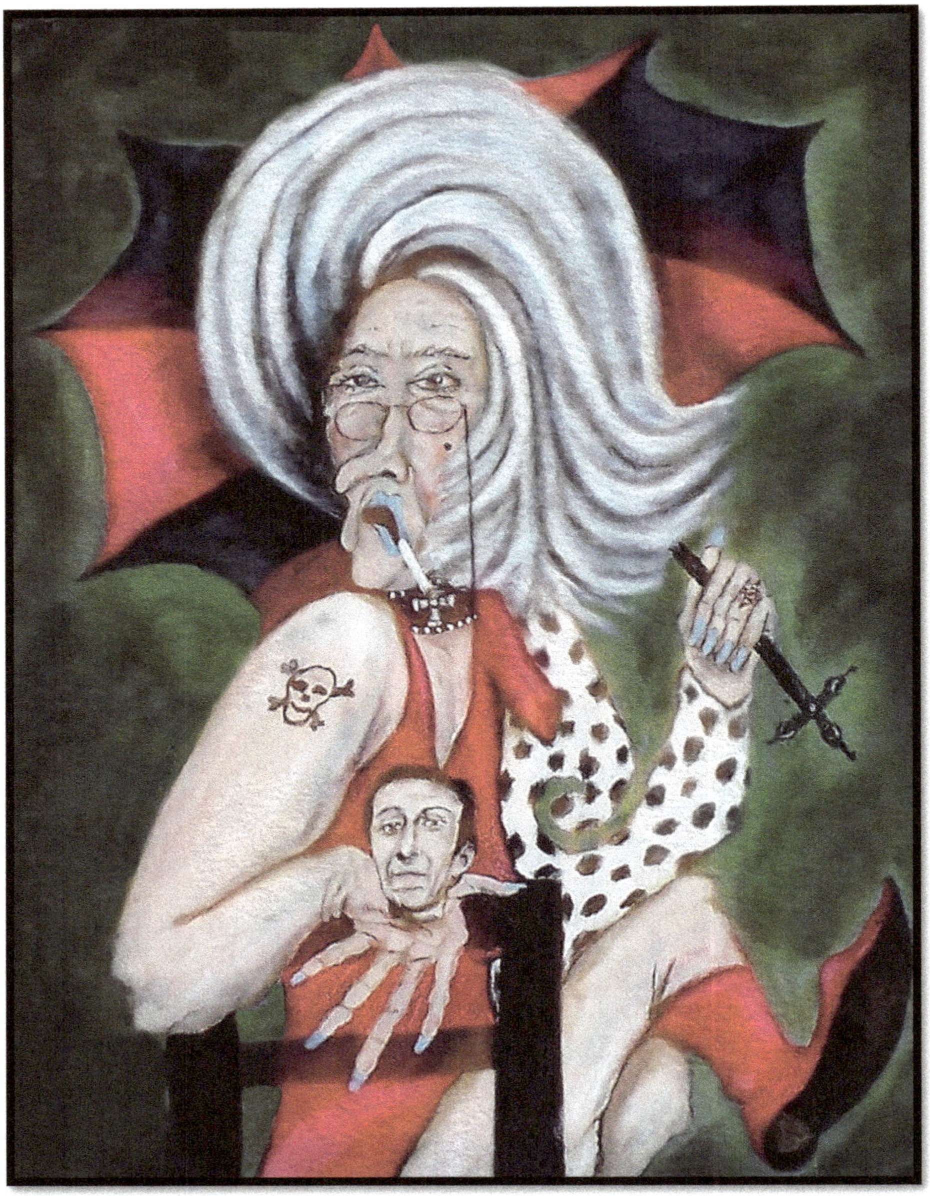

HOW MRS. CLAUS LOST IT ALL

Mrs. Claus grew tired of Santa,
His laws and wooly jaws,
So, she beheaded his tattletale elf,
Who wouldn't get off her shelf,
And she moved to New Orleans by fall.
But when the "*ho-ho-hos*" quit coming,
And she ran out of toys and money,
She took a job in a red-lit stall.

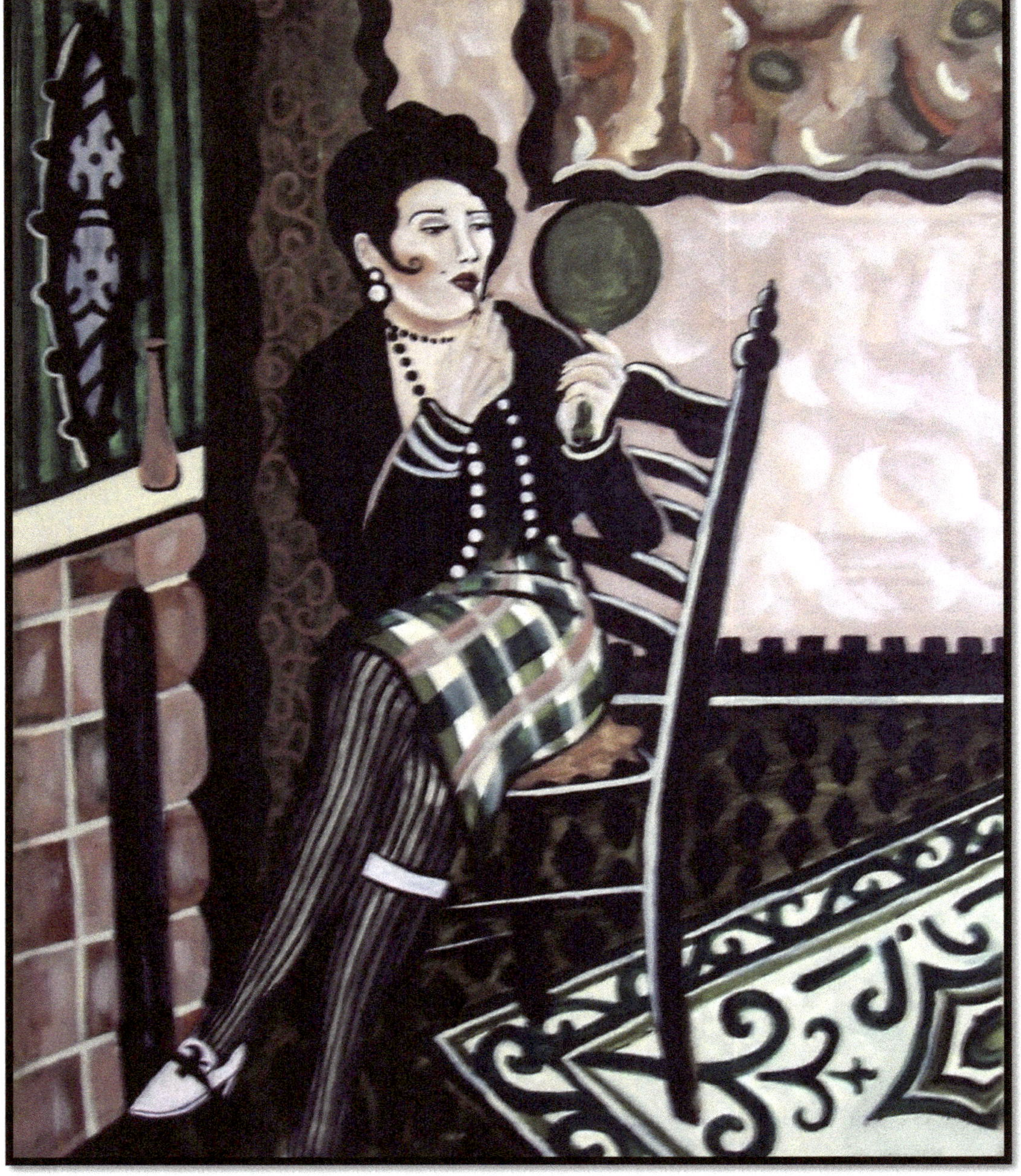

THE LIMBO TANGO - OTHERWISE KNOWN AS THE FLAPPER FLOPPER

In the twilight of what's left of sleep,
When life's a bubble against grief and defeat,
Did you ever imagine you would realize
Times have changed?
You wasted it when you had it.
Nothing stays the same.
You were so close, but at most, it was in vain.
And the new just won't do, but it's stuck like glue,
Like a tune a few call cool.
And those golden moments, the gods are now withholding,
Were just tokens bestowed upon you.
Left in limbo,
Inside you know there's a diamond glow,
But the world will never know,
Only you.

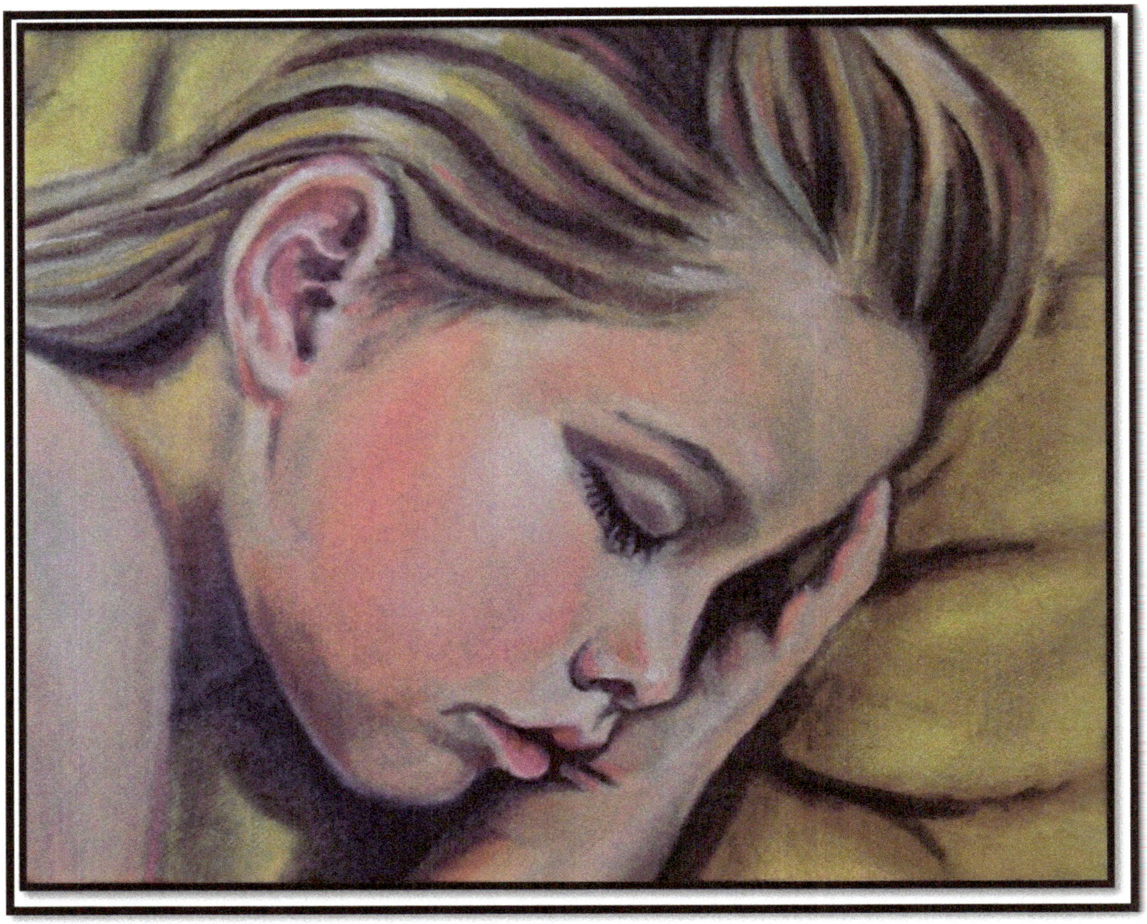

AFTER THE UMBILICAL VEIN WANES, THE BIRTH DEPT REMAINS

Some people don't see children as humans
Who will someday weigh their deeds,
Produce receipts of their hypocrisy
After their souls bleed,
After their keepers' needs are spent.
Youth non-returnable.
Indeed,
They are flowers wilted before ever blooming.

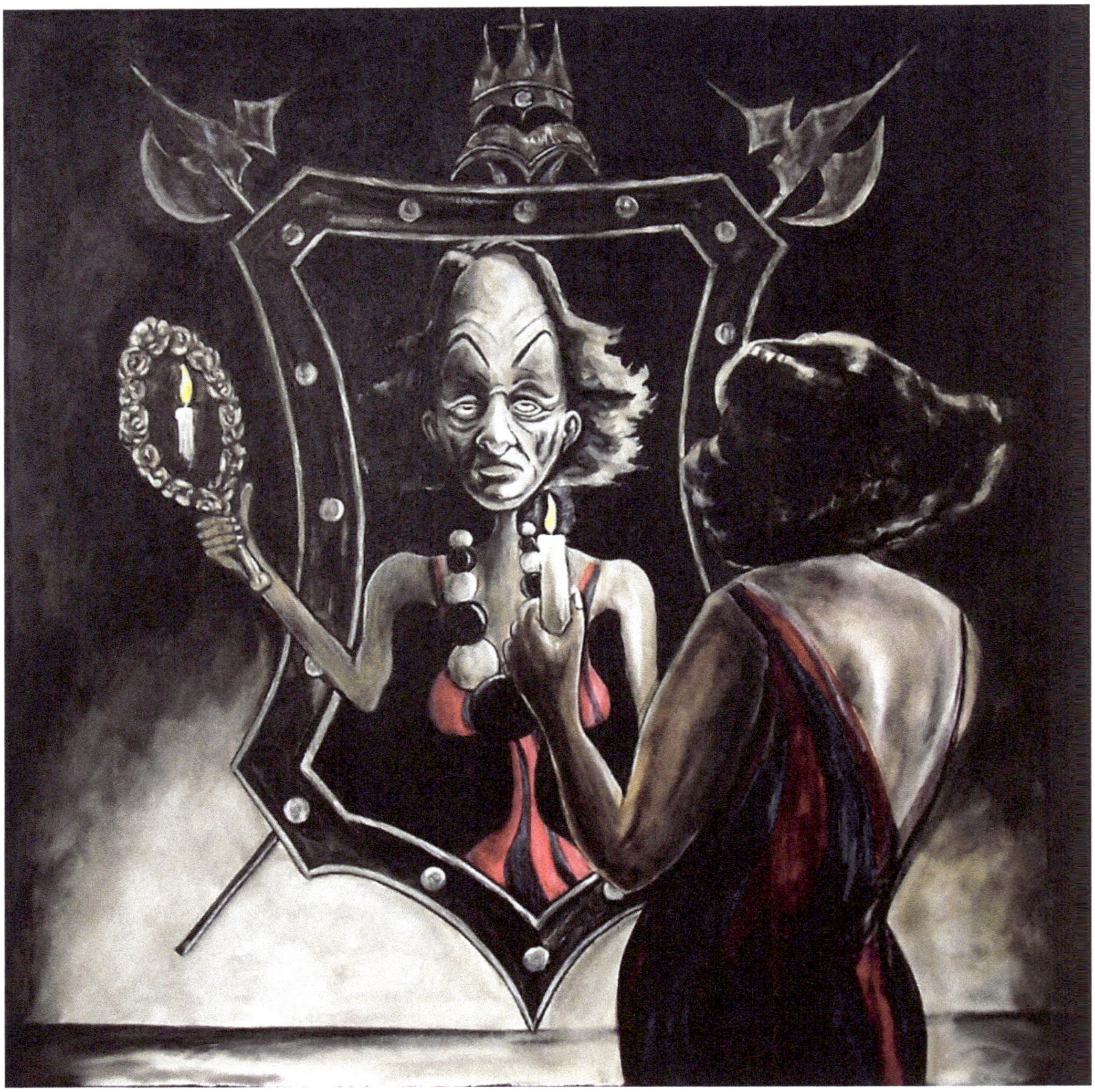

ILLUSIONS AND PERCEPTIONS

"Protective shield on the wall,
Whose reflection is young and tall?"
The old battle-ax stands to fall,
Because her new flame isn't real at all.

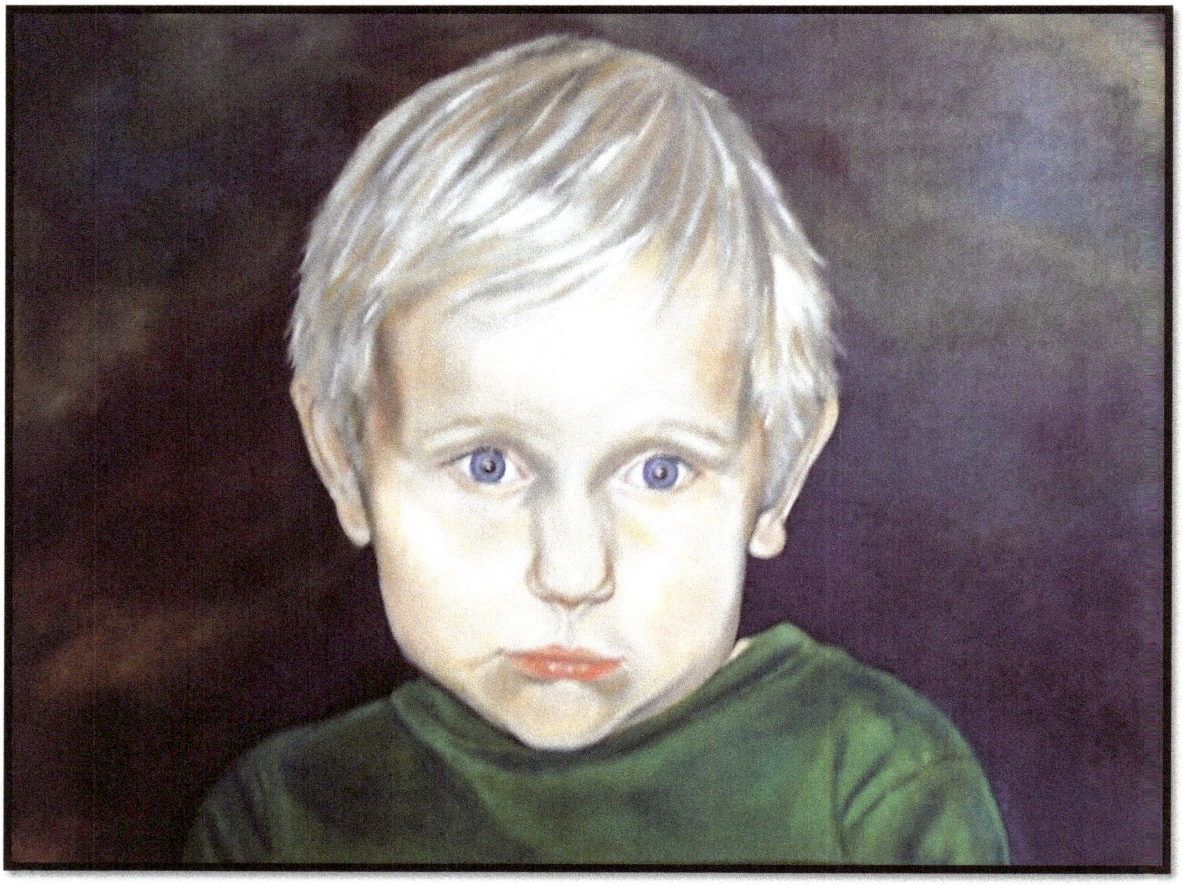

LITTLE BILLY DIY

Mother knew it was too quiet in the house.
Little Billy was always rambunctious and wild
Unless he was being a particularly naughty child,
Thinking no one could see him acting so mild,
Sneaking around the attic and shadowy nooks
With his Fix-It-Yourself coloring books.

She ran through the hallway, and to her surprise,
He had plugged in her blender full of Daddy's neckties.
"Oh, Billy, oh, Billy!" she stammered and shook,
And unplugged the electric cord, giving him a look.

Billy's lip pooched as he thought of excuses.
With Mama's temper, it was utterly useless.
"But I was helping make dinner," he sniffled and cried,
And gazed at the floor with sad little eyes.

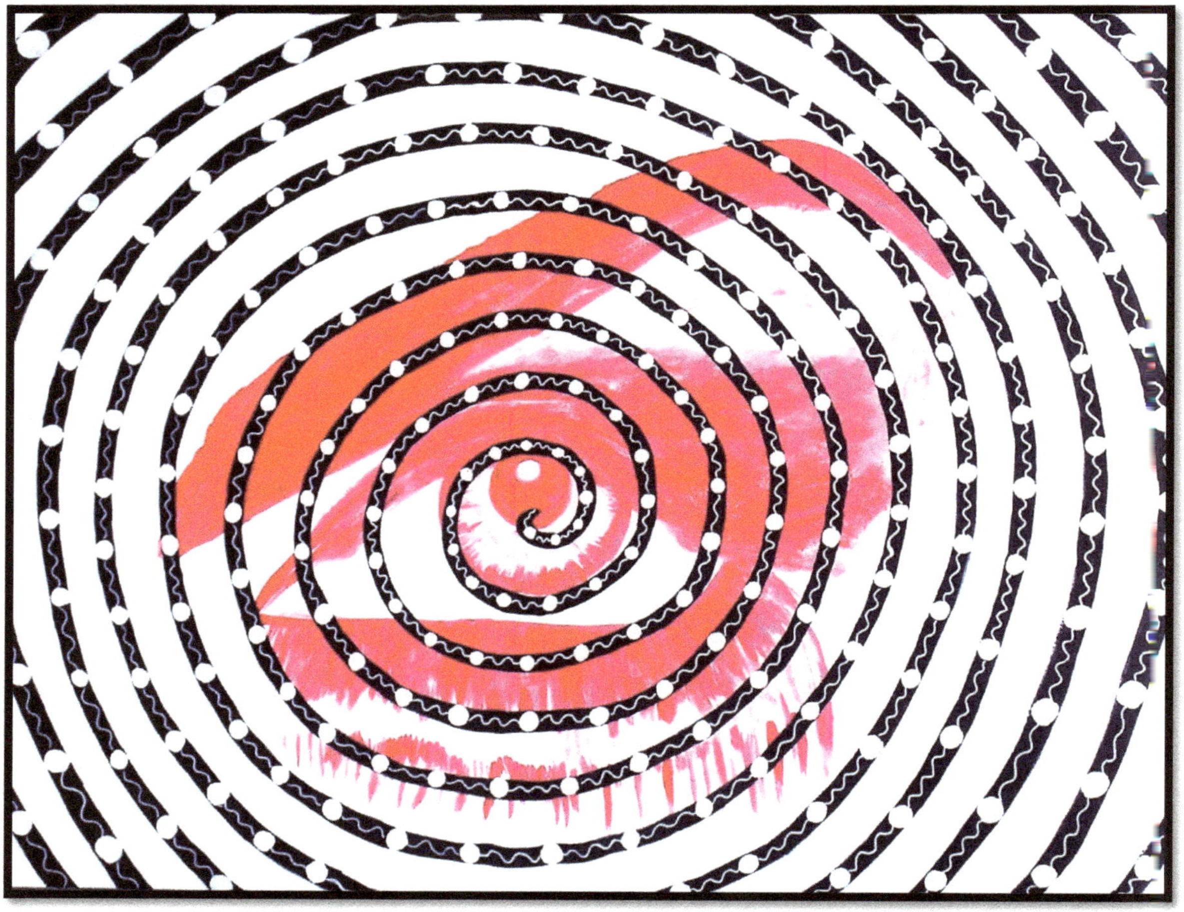

IN SYNC

Across the rink,
She struck a boundary pose in scarlet clothes.
Undeterred, his right brow rose.
Why would she not wink?
He would break through. Indeed, he knew
She was the only one he would pursue.
Drunken by her beauty,
Rescuing her was his duty,
For a field of weeds was no place for a rose.

She whisked right on by;
The wind on her dress caressed her thigh.
She had had enough of fly-by-night promises
And sympathy to make her a doubting Thomas.
Once cornered, he lifted her to the sky.
And only then did she surrender.
For now, nothing could be denied.

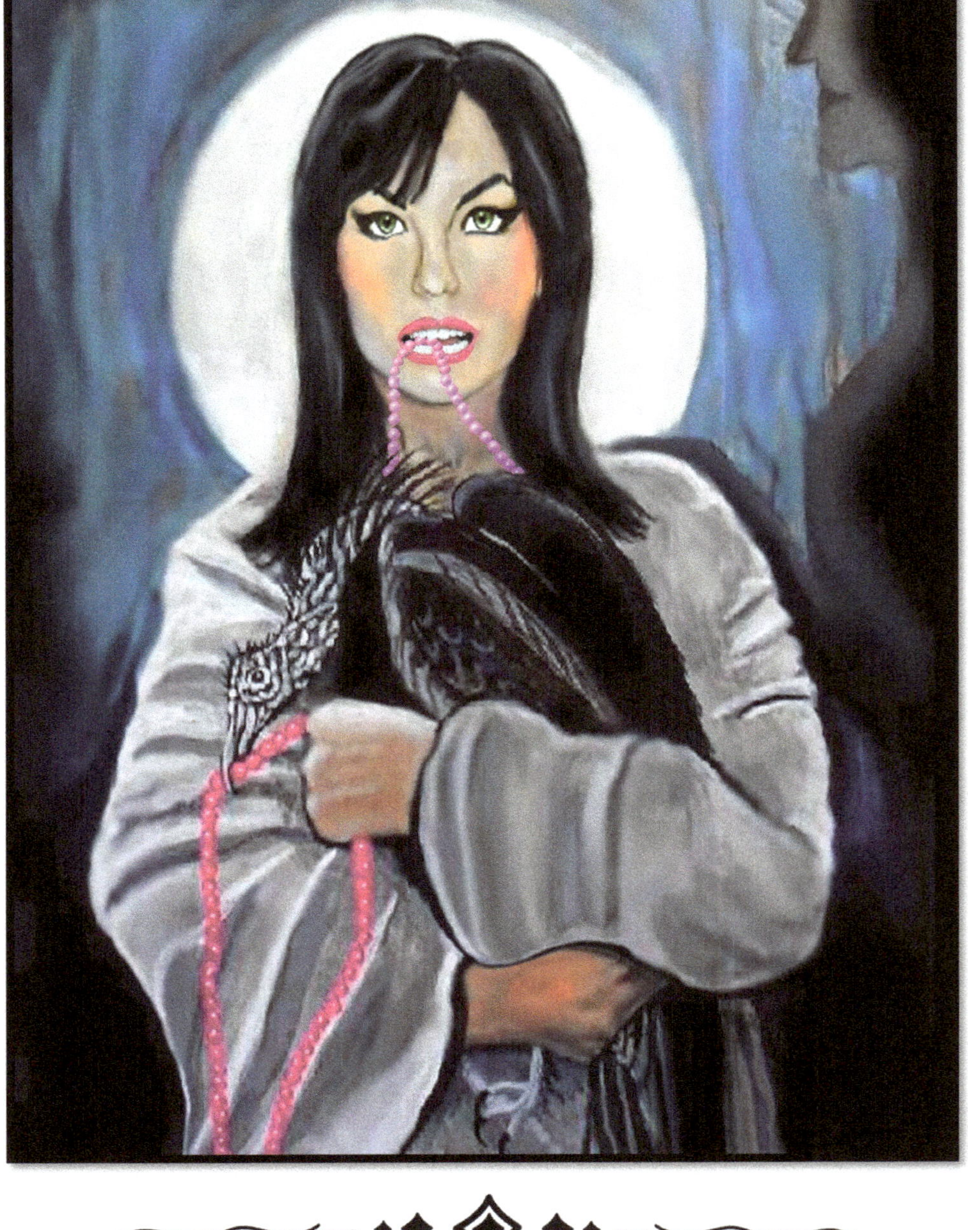

MISJUDGED MALEIA MEDITATING IN THE MEADOW

When the moon is full, and the leaves are lacy,
MaLeia beckons her buzzard to her sweet embraces.
Some say to keep such a pet is extreme and reckless,
For they reckon it eats carrion and dead things with faces.
But MaLeia knows as she spoons it with praises
That it only eats beads on her pink pearly necklace.

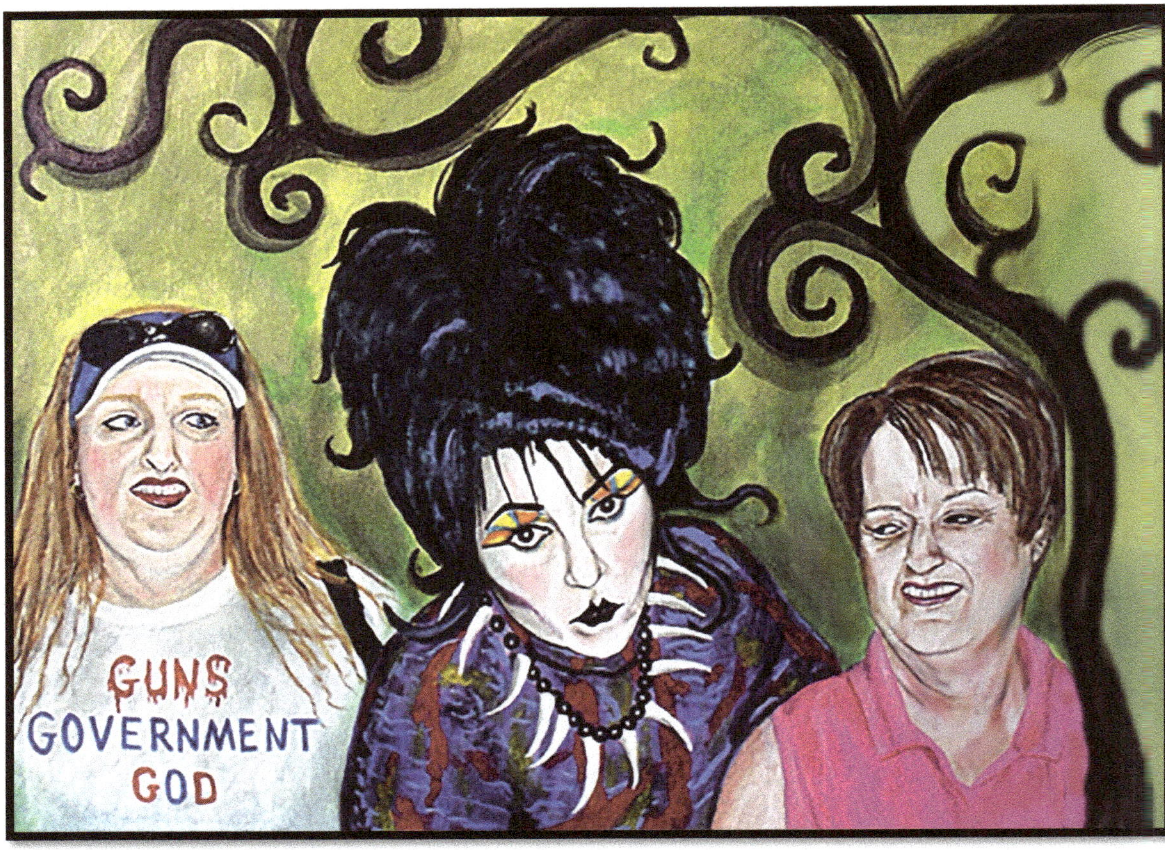
GUNS
GOVERNMENT
GOD

MINGLE LIMBO

The atmosphere turned toxic
As the root of disdain spread its noxious tendrils.
Smiles became caustic.
Beguiled by all that's identical,
The crowd began to dwindle.
They gathered in their boxes,
Spewing gossip like a faucet.
Caustic closet.
Same old flames ever to rekindle.
Talking to themselves. Talking to a mirror.

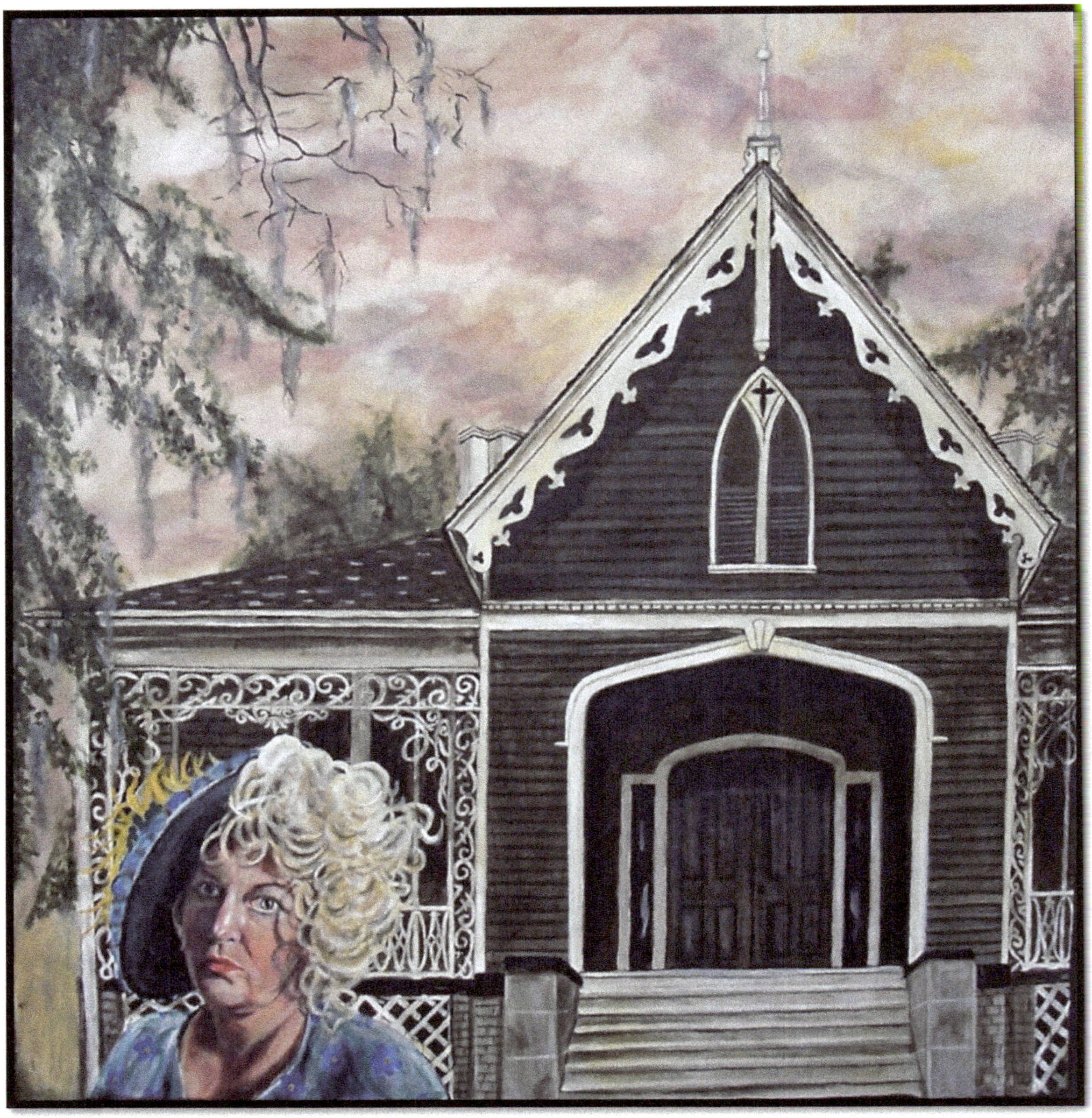

MS. MAYZIE HAD A FLUFFY

James used to pull the car around
For Ms. Mayzie to get to town.
So, she painted on a frown and called a taxi,
But it put on the gas and drove right past her.
In fact, she never saw a car crash any faster.
Just the day before, there had been ten cows in her pasture,
And daily sermons from her pesky old pastor.
No, today she walked past a new pile of steel,
Sipping a desperate glass of milk,
Reciting "Thou shalt not kill."

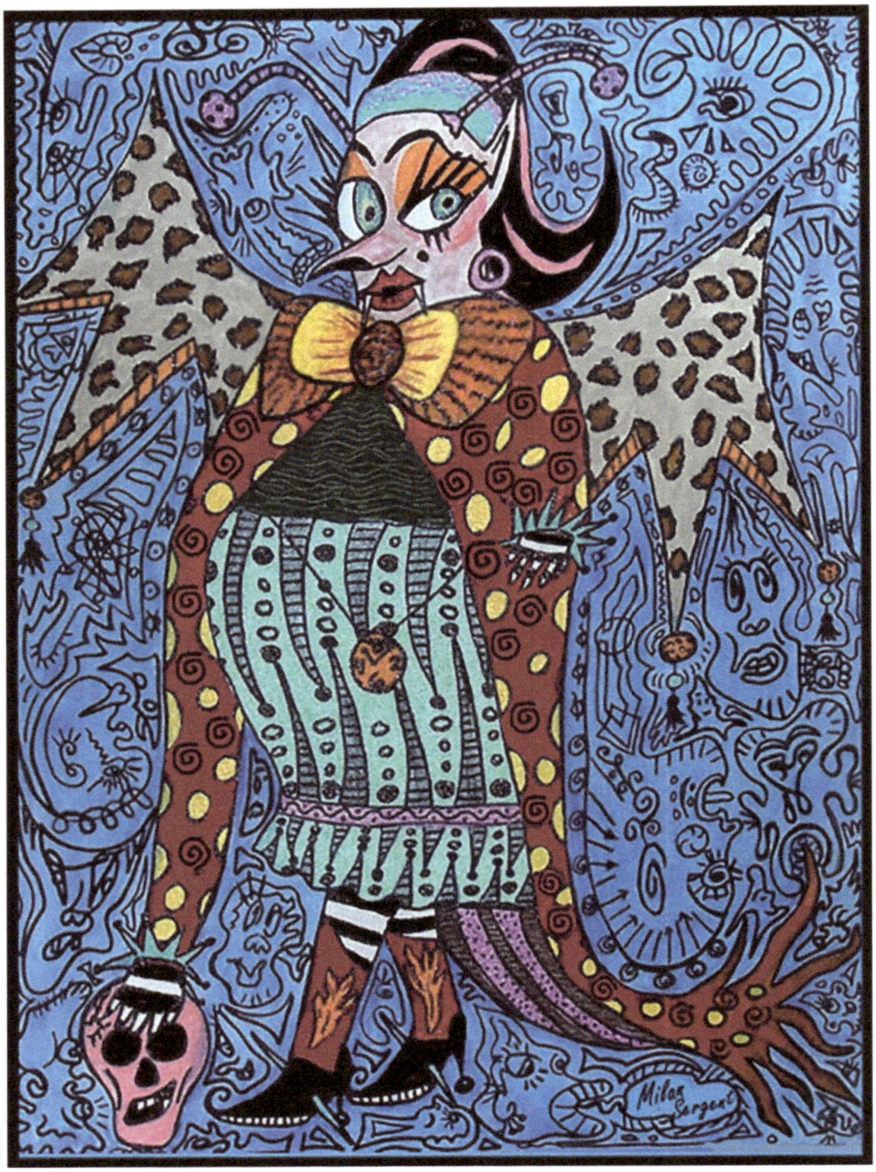
Milan Sargent

NIGHT OF THE LIVING DEB

Night of the living Deb
crawled from under the bed.
She's a thirsty mosquito.
"Not too good with people,"
Once said her ex named Fred.

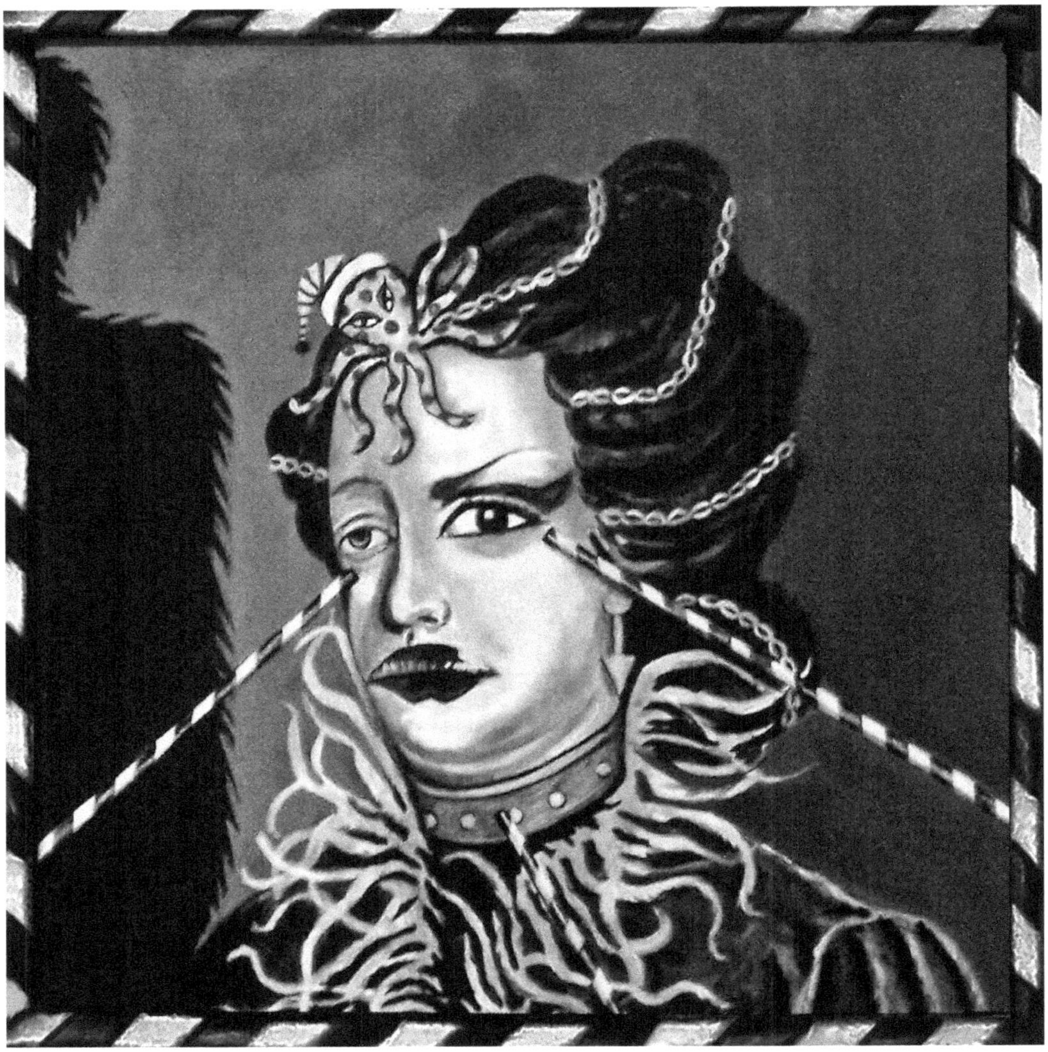

NITPICKERS ANONYMOUS

Shackled, Pursey put on a pucker
while tackled by his bettors.

"Oh my! He has a painted smile and eye? It can't be hidden," said Nitpickers Anonymous, cracking their pointers on Pursey's imperfections: a scrutinizing obsession for the inquisitors' delight.

"It's my smile you knocked upside-down, and the bruise you left on my lid."

"Well, it matches your necklace. Precious, Pursey."

"It's a fetter, and it's hurting," he sighed.

"And do tell — is that frilly fringe upon your lapel?"

"Certainly not. It is tendrils unraveled from the straitjackets you sell."

"Don't deny the bracelets crowning your matted mane."

"Face it! They're chains you affixed to constrain my brain. And let's get this straight: No earring pierces my lobe; it's your tag to show what I am and which direction my soul will go."

"So? It shouldn't be that hard to tell for us

who are obviously your betters. You're unhappy. *That's* a big teller."

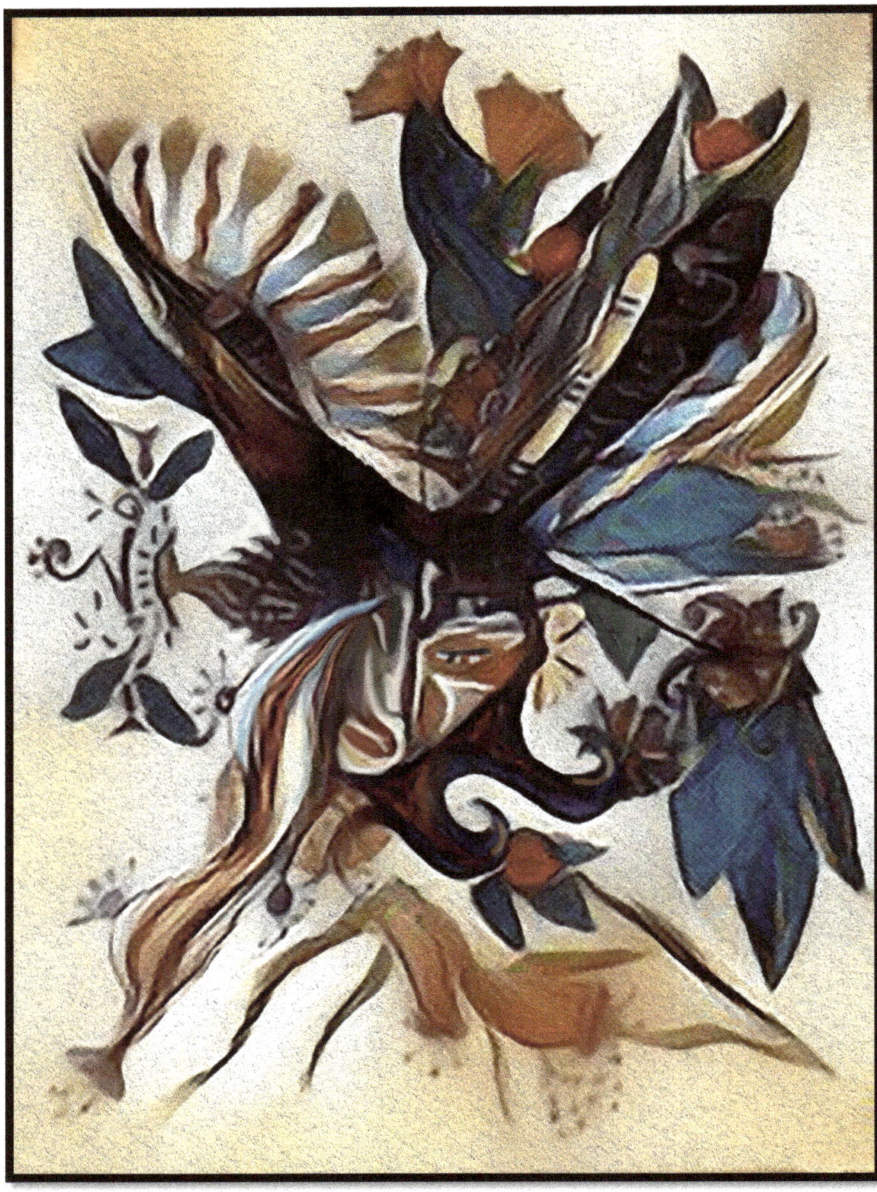

NOW ONLY NATURE KNOWS

Yon eve, the windswept prints dead on the lonely stroll
Decaying, ripe for spring's green reorder.
Tracks once deep, shared, for their love,
Incompared, once deemed complete,
Form sand, sustaining teary rain
Under tissues of leaves along yen's border,
Awaiting the breeze, wishing time grew slower.
If the roots of the trees, the shoots, and the bulbs
Could, in a synthesis no photo could restore,
Resurrect amore's stored harmony — now only a stain,
On the indigenous street, and in the peeps of the sparrows
Nesting in branches so steep,
Kindling rekindling their need,
Repair the pair complete.

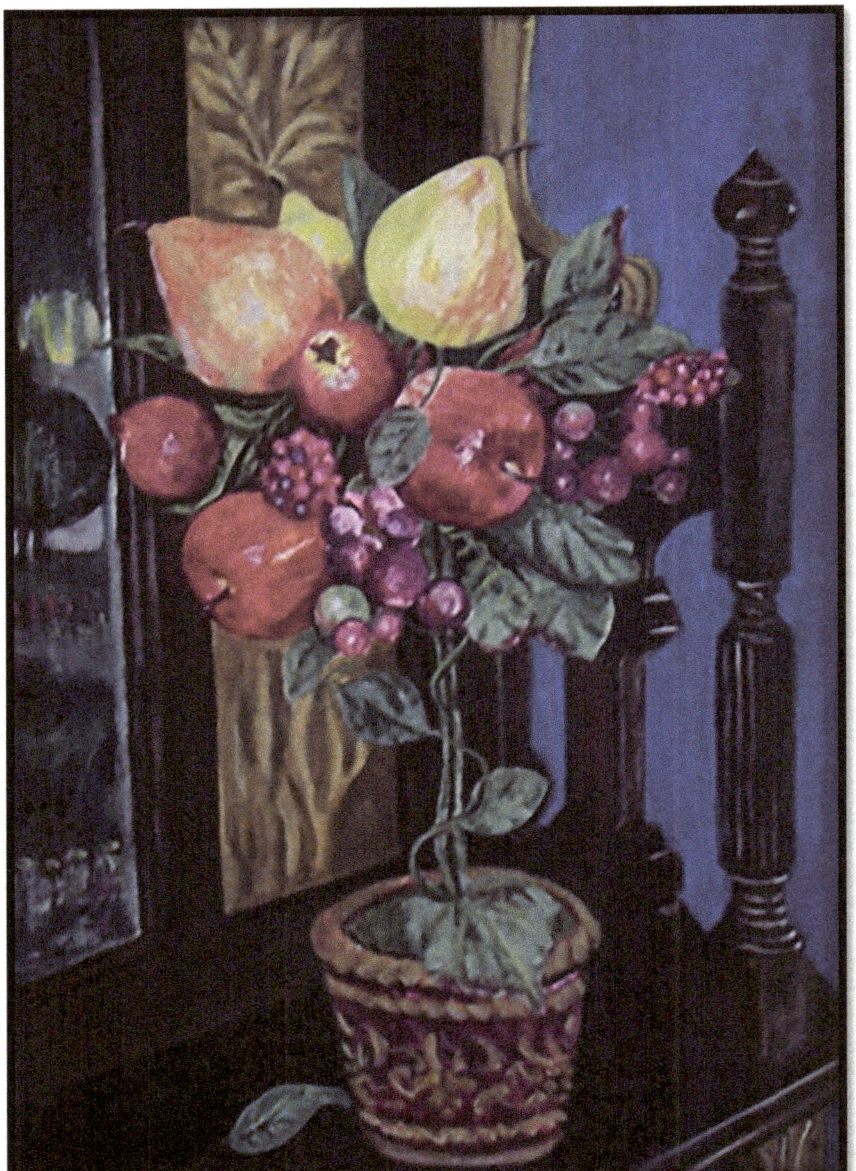

MAGIC APPLES GROWN BY THE WRONG AUTHOR MUST BE IGNORED

Spoon-fed children become spoon-fed adults.
With ripe orchards by the host,
They swallow rotten apples while offering up a toast.
Though there's a catacomb of history,
It causes their conscious misery,
So, they retain and proclaim select moments the most.
Shutting their eyes to the billions,
They give their conscience to a ghost.
Rationing realities while shunning variety,
Their brains programmed on fulfilling
Such things that they boast.

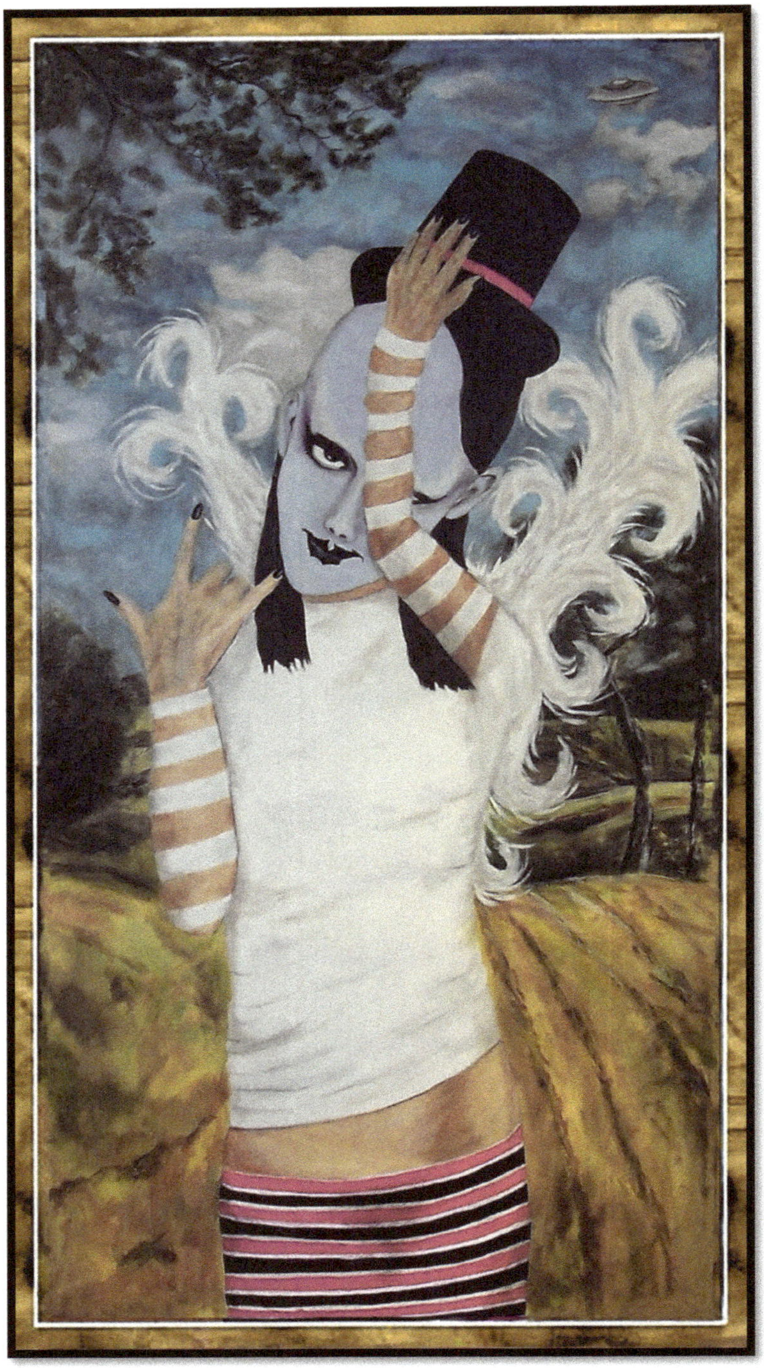

QUESTIONABLE EXTRATERRESTRIALS

Crop circles on pastures.
Increasing reptilian features.
Are they disk-riding Watchers
Or interplanetary teachers?
Chip-implanting drones
With broken-off wings?
Soon we will meet
The little, gray-skinned beings
With top hats and designer jeans,
And three fingers held up
In the sign of peace.

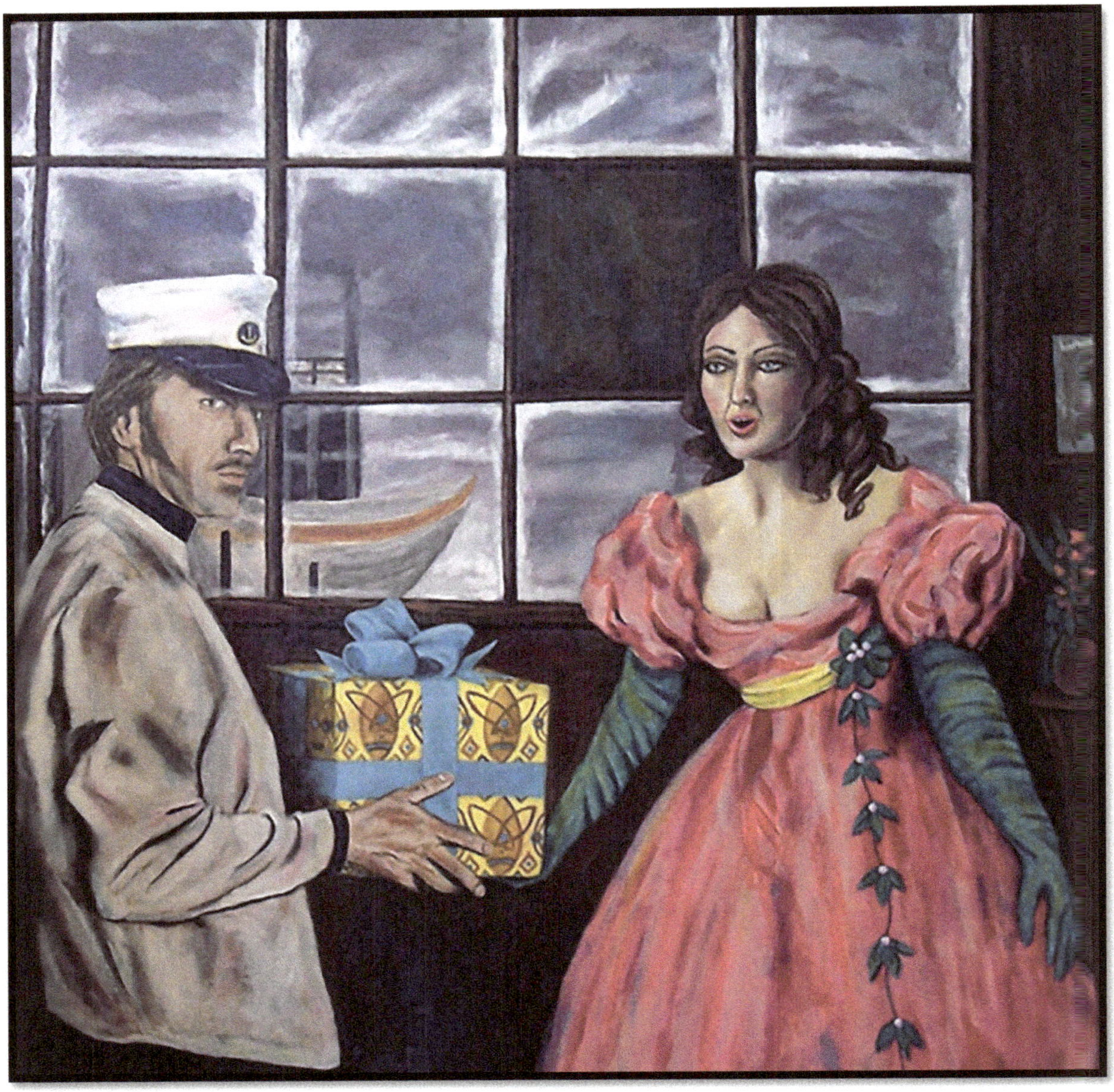

RAGE AND GLORY

Far from her latticed galleries and mansionry callers,
Brandy's new life ticked in eons while eyeing the harbor,
Waiting on crates and barrels and promised tomorrows.
Gifted forgiveness eventually came
From her captain with a shifty grin and no name.
So much for refrain and showers in a leaky warehouse rain.
Brandy found only rage in its beribboned glory.
And he rambled far too long with his sailor stories.

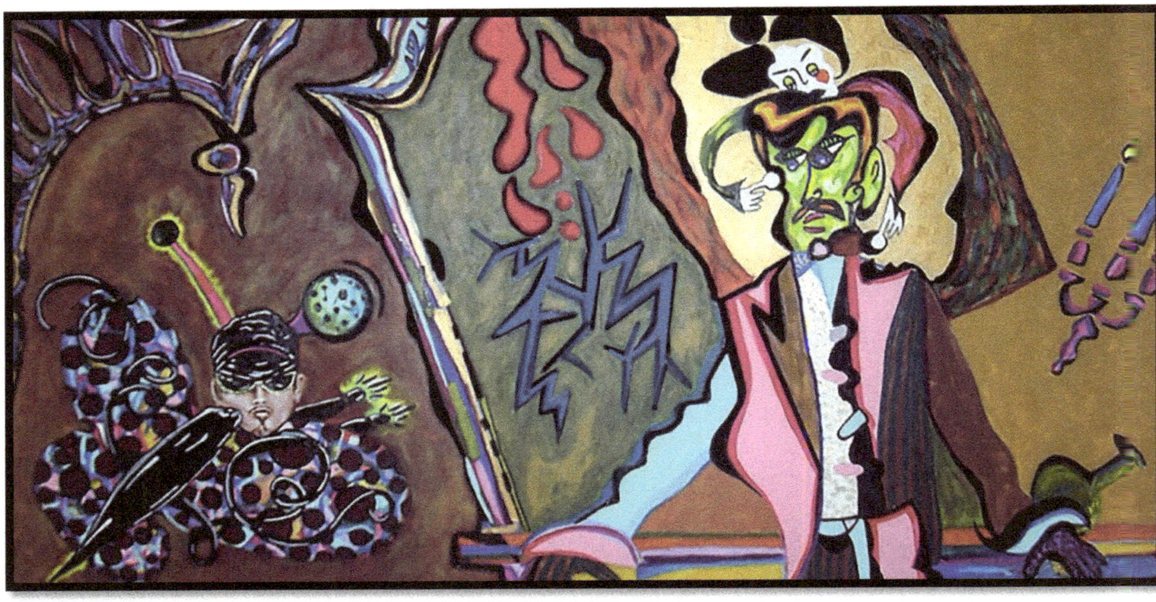

SHIFTY GIFTING

Don't hold your breath
At the permanence of wrapped presents
Or the sparkling sincerity before your eyes
When it proves to be mud pies.
The bulk of which is selfish stock,
Insurance for the investors' plots.
Never wonder what you've done
To become the abandoned one.
I give you a valuable tip:
Don't bother to open a single gift.
For when it has run its course,
It was just a Trojan Horse.

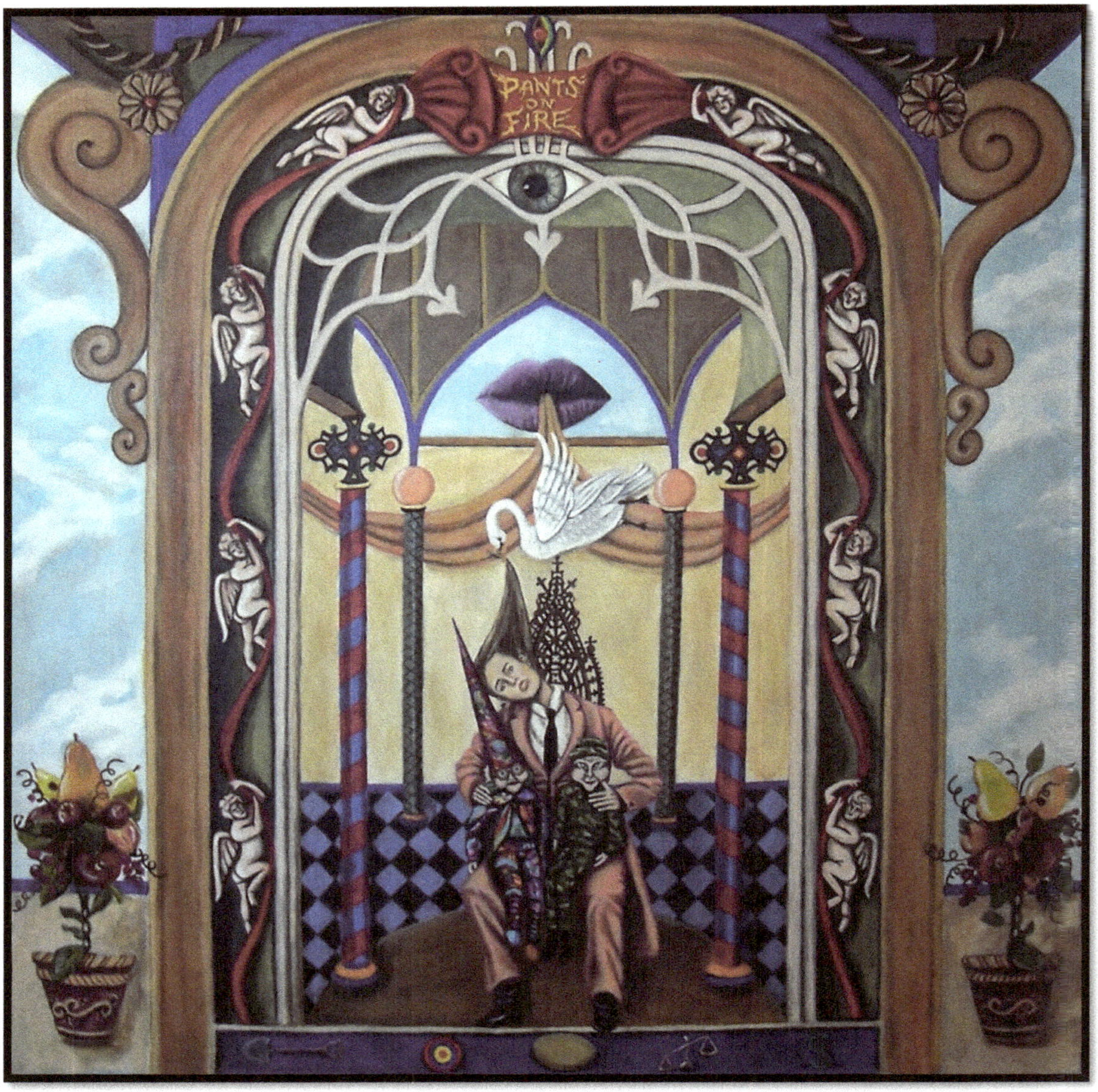
PANTS
ON
FIRE

PANTS ON FIRE

Liar, liar, refocus your vision.
Your veneer of indifference, once dewdrops dripping,
Has now become a torrential flood of recognition.

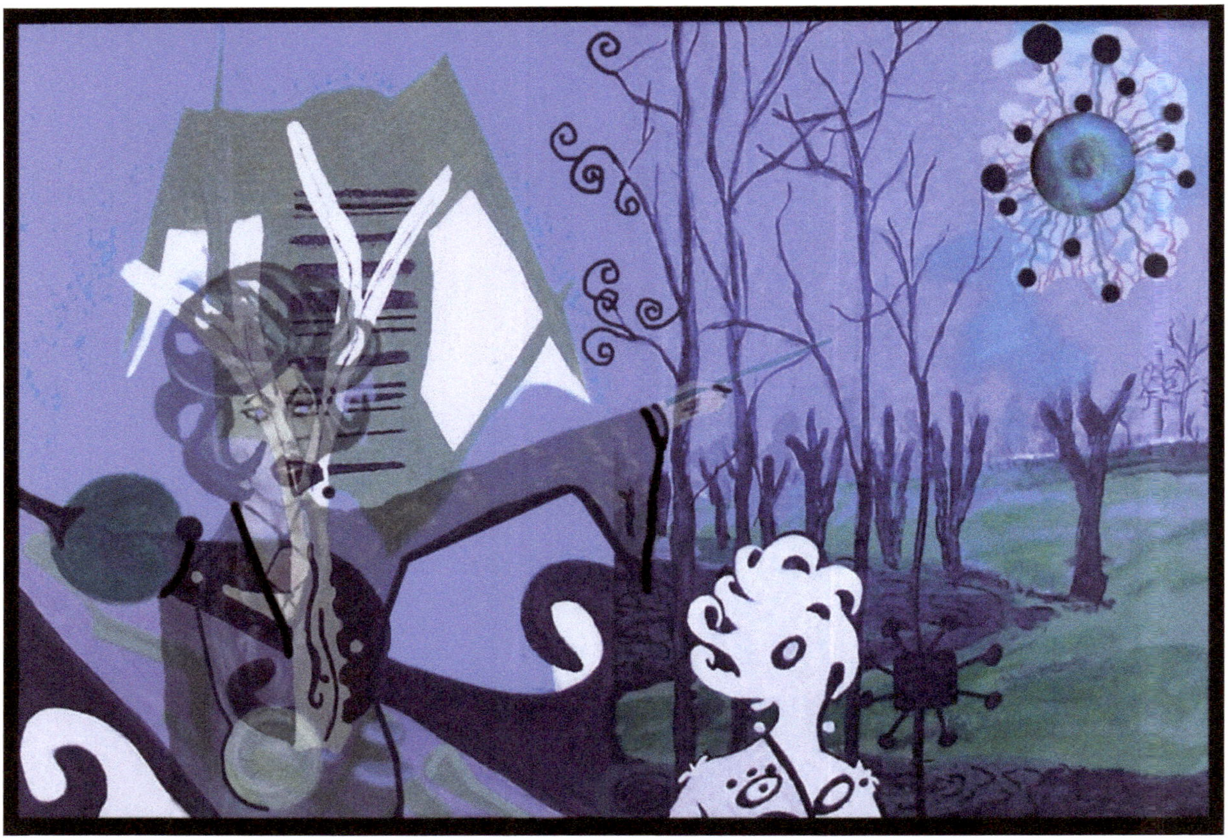

SADIE

Sadie always says events categorized as nucleosynthesis
Are no natural coincidences.
Quantum psychics exist in the physical,
But she lives in the mental.
More than pancontinental,
A light among concentric circles,
Nested spheres because you're not really there
And she's not here.
She is fetching silver threads across the firmament.
Traversing each realm, she knits astral webs with bliss.
The temple sheltering the third eye
Speaks
A continual prophecy.
Words are still squeezing betwixt her teeth.
Sadie never needs beauty sleep.
She's getting a predetermined make-over on Déjà Vu Street,
A true permanent.

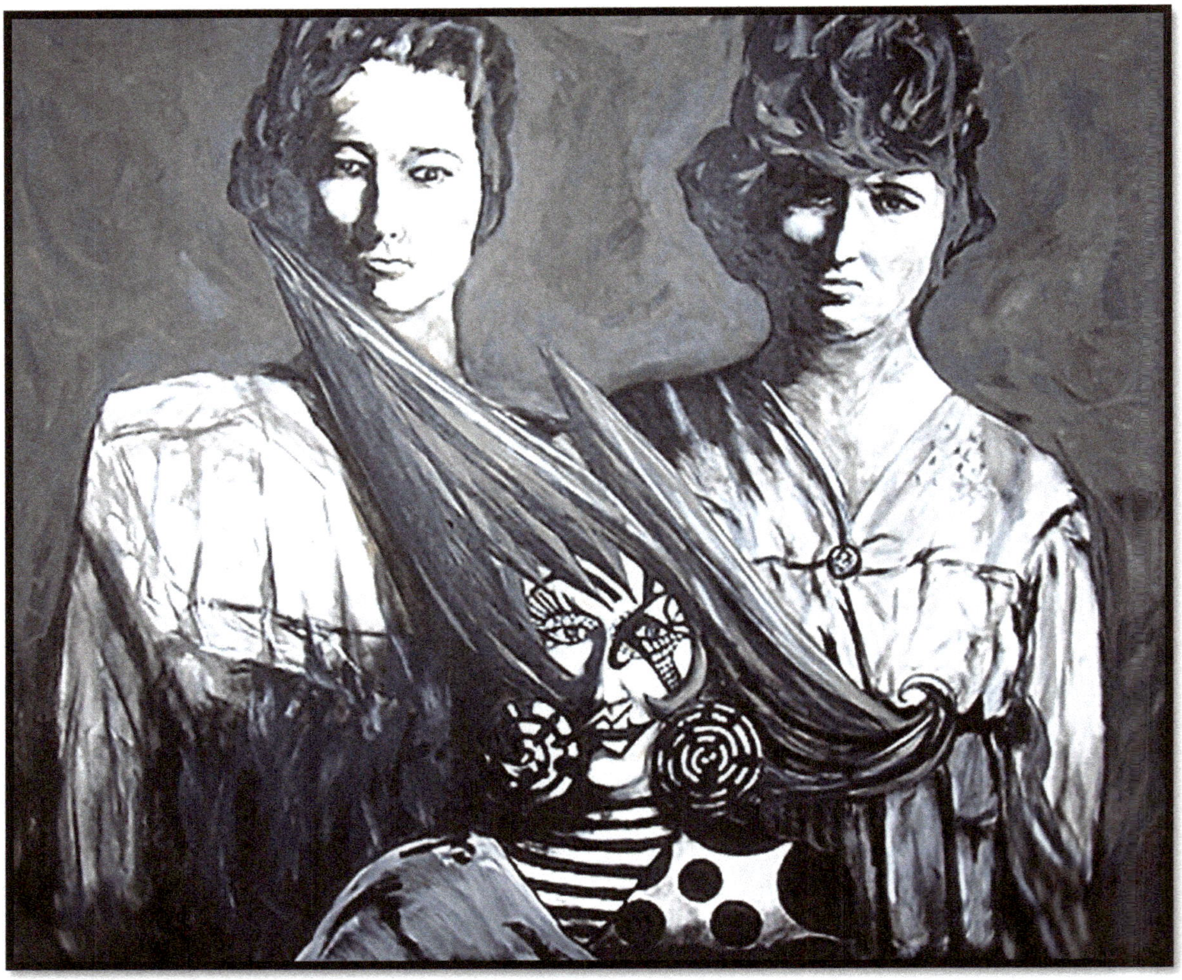

OVER THE SHOULDER SCOLDERS OF THOSE WHO ARE BOLDER

When the kissers amid ya look weaned on a pickle,
And their glares harden as if you are fickle,
Never make wishes that you'll start blending.
'Tis the others who obviously need more offending.
If such unique things make their skin green,
Then their borders need expanding.
Life is too short to bore stars who are born.
Maybe it's the haters who ought to conform.

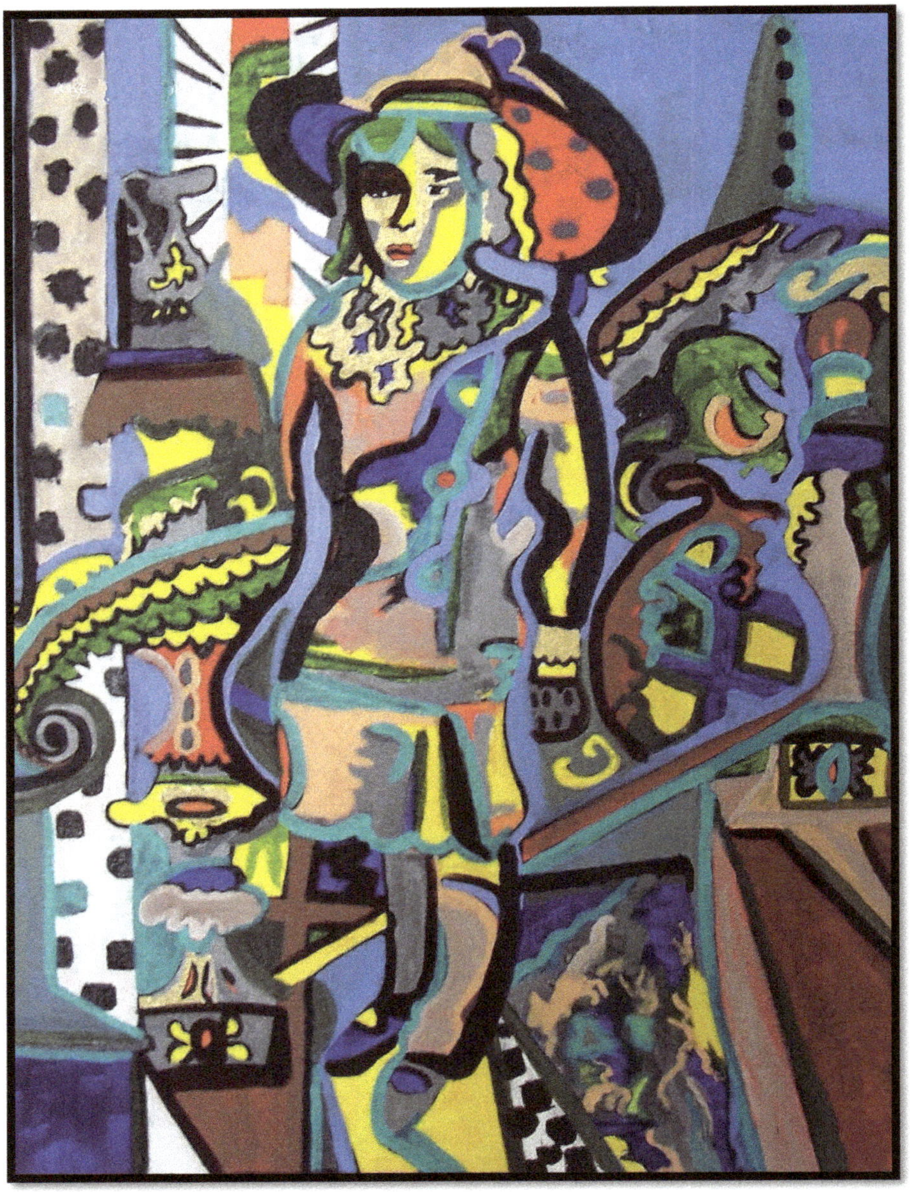

SHE'S INVISIBLE NOW

Faded like a phantom intent.
Warbled words one truly meant.
Discarded after the parting of the lips.
Out of sight means never missed.
This is a wallflower's bitter bliss.
What might've been if she ever went?
Camouflaged in an absentee list.
Her cloistered conclusions are fantasies spent.

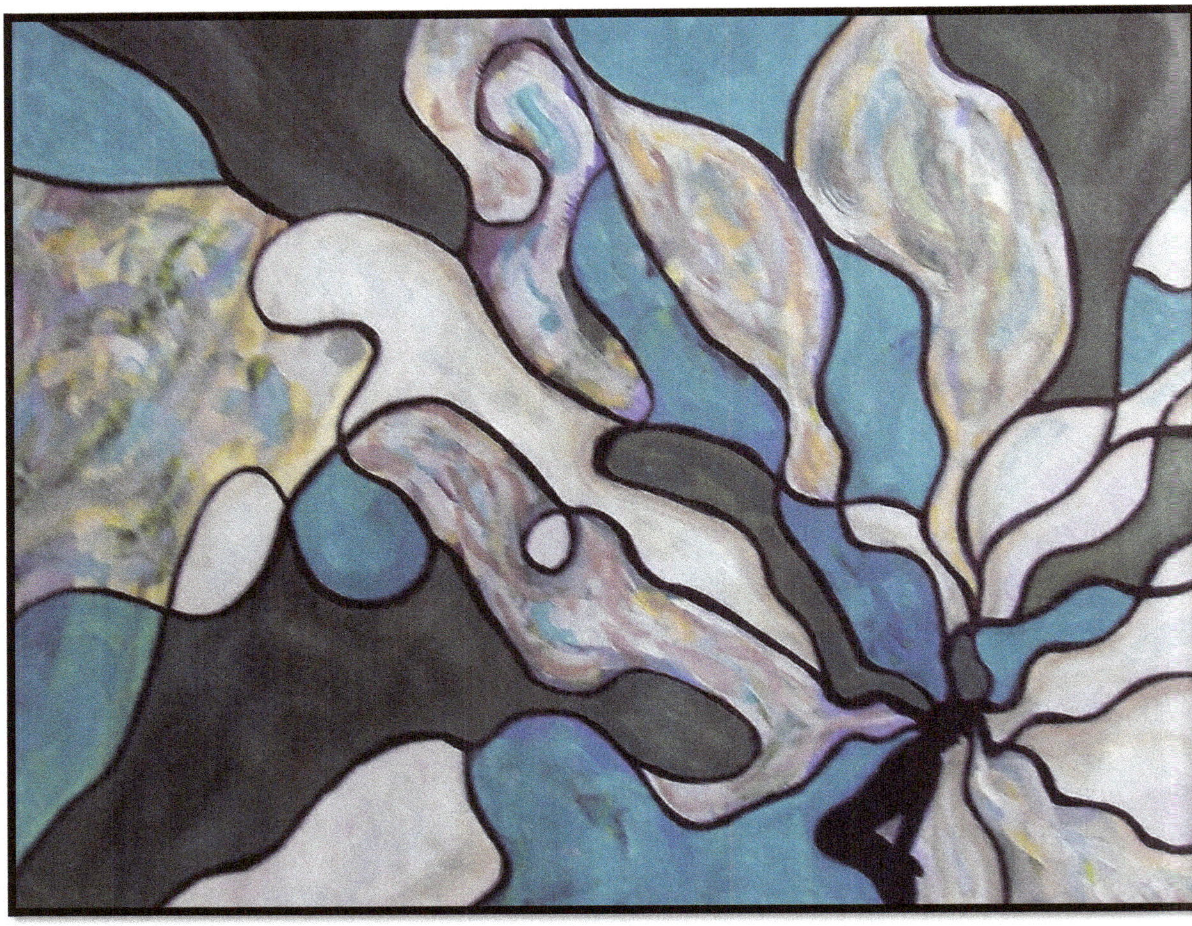

TIME HAS A FUNNY WAY

Am I the only one who digs up graves?
At least in my thoughts from far away.
How pitiful I must be to seek
Life among the dead, for they are the ones
Who have long ago buried me.
How absurd I am to think they would seek me.
What have I done to have set myself free?
Did I move one block too far?
Change jobs, hair, religion, or cause?
Should I have taken that nap?
Is that where the years vanished
And all was lost?
Or am I better off a lonely wretch
Whose only memories of them are kept?

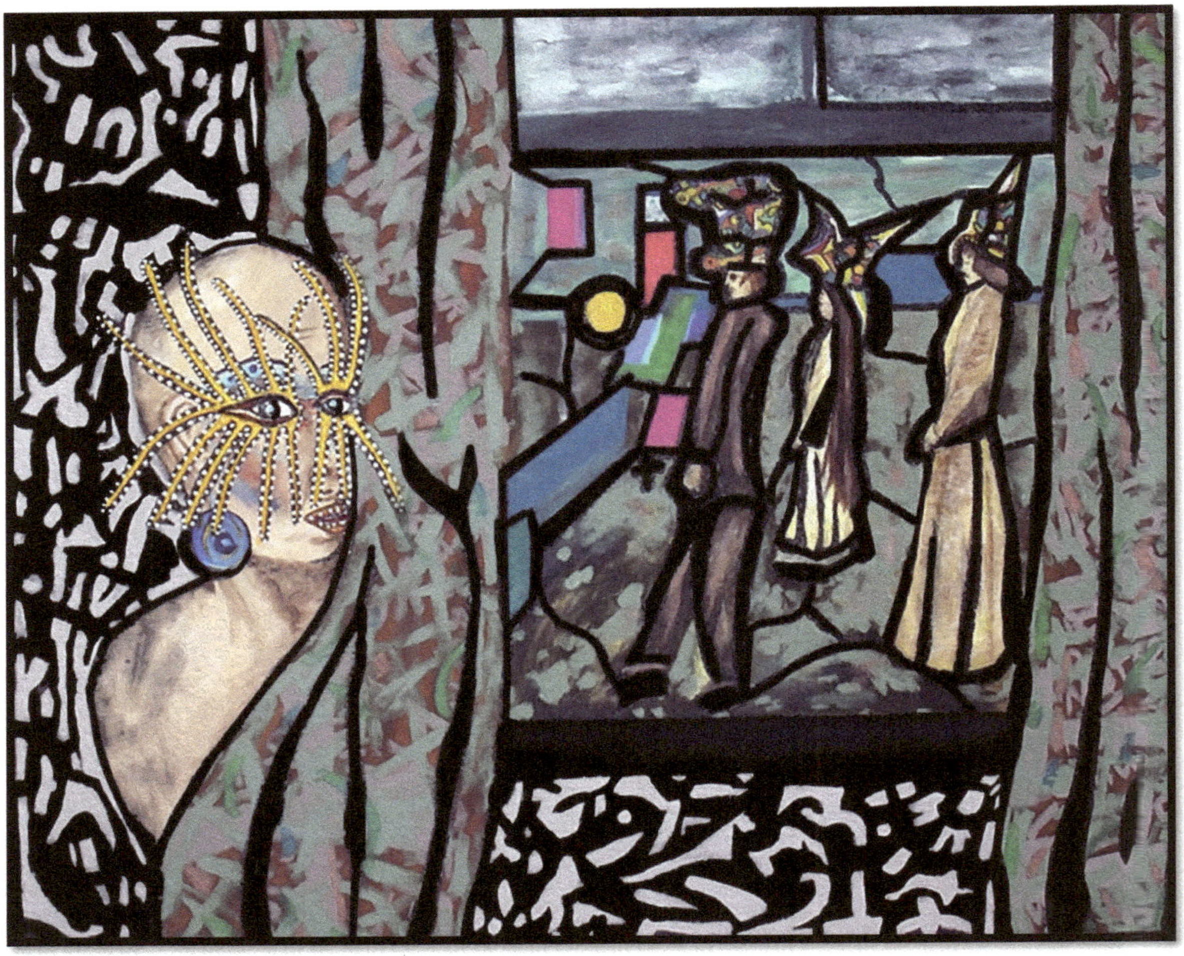

COMMUNAL "YOU KNOWS"

I write in riddles because of the stealth of my home
In a belt where many were hung.
A place deep, trapped — never I wanted to be.
Among the clones.
My true voice alienates me further than I already am.
Alone.
Here, the tribal unspokenness has been honed to a high level
A knowing.
With a simple question, the phrase catchers can
Spot any dissension showing.
They secretly long for another revolution
A "cleansing."
I want to vomit on these seemingly good
Spoon-feds being humans.
Their selective judgments are considered "winning."
But the end is like the beginning,
An ism of dominion now supported by whispers.

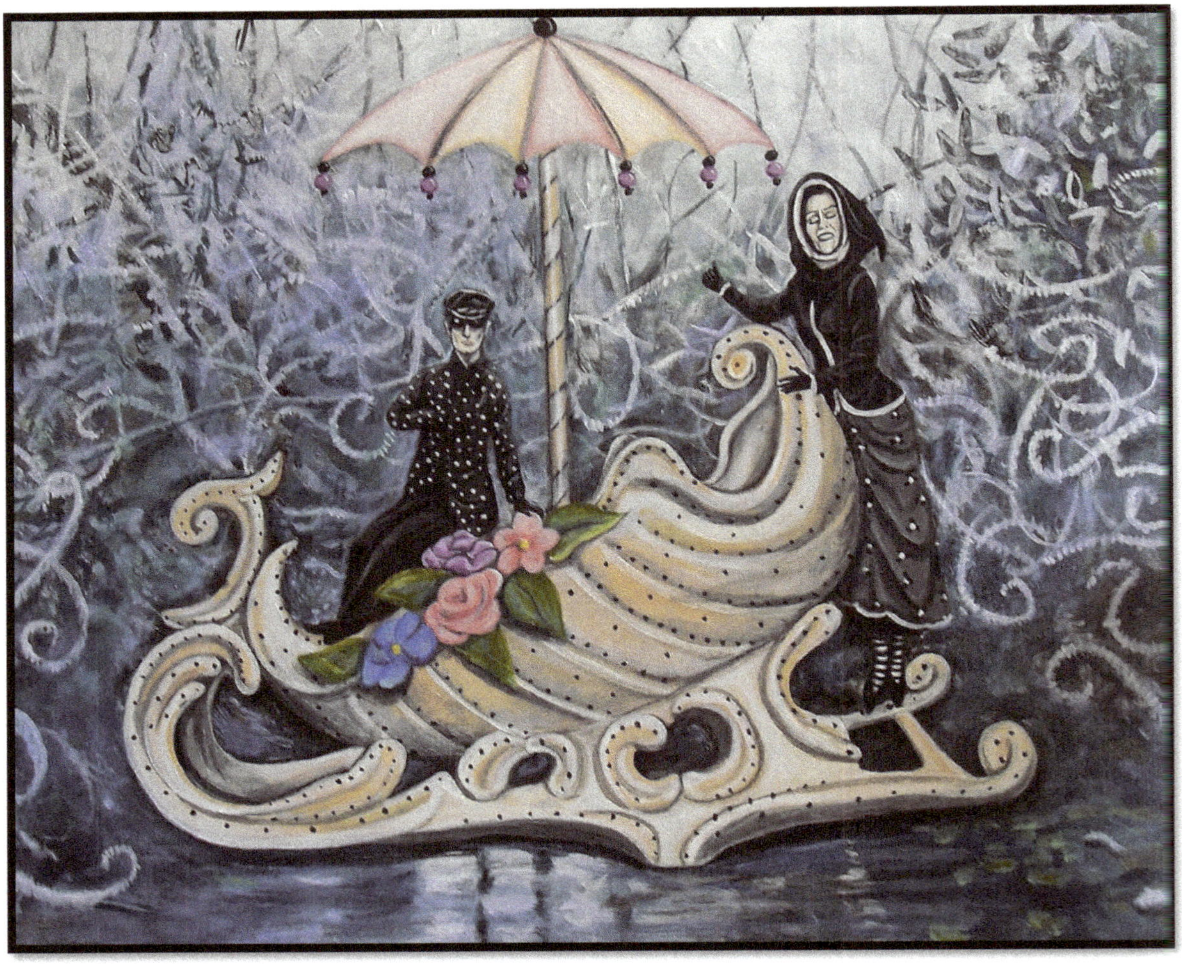

SLEIGH-BOAT OF HOPE

Occasionally, when drifting over Bayou Brahms,
The tree-lined bank parted its foreboding curtains
As the sun's glistening indulgence danced
Across the icy swamp.
The air grew thinner, eclipsing reality.
Though their innate natures, be they ever so quickening,
Hadn't thawed their frozen mentality.

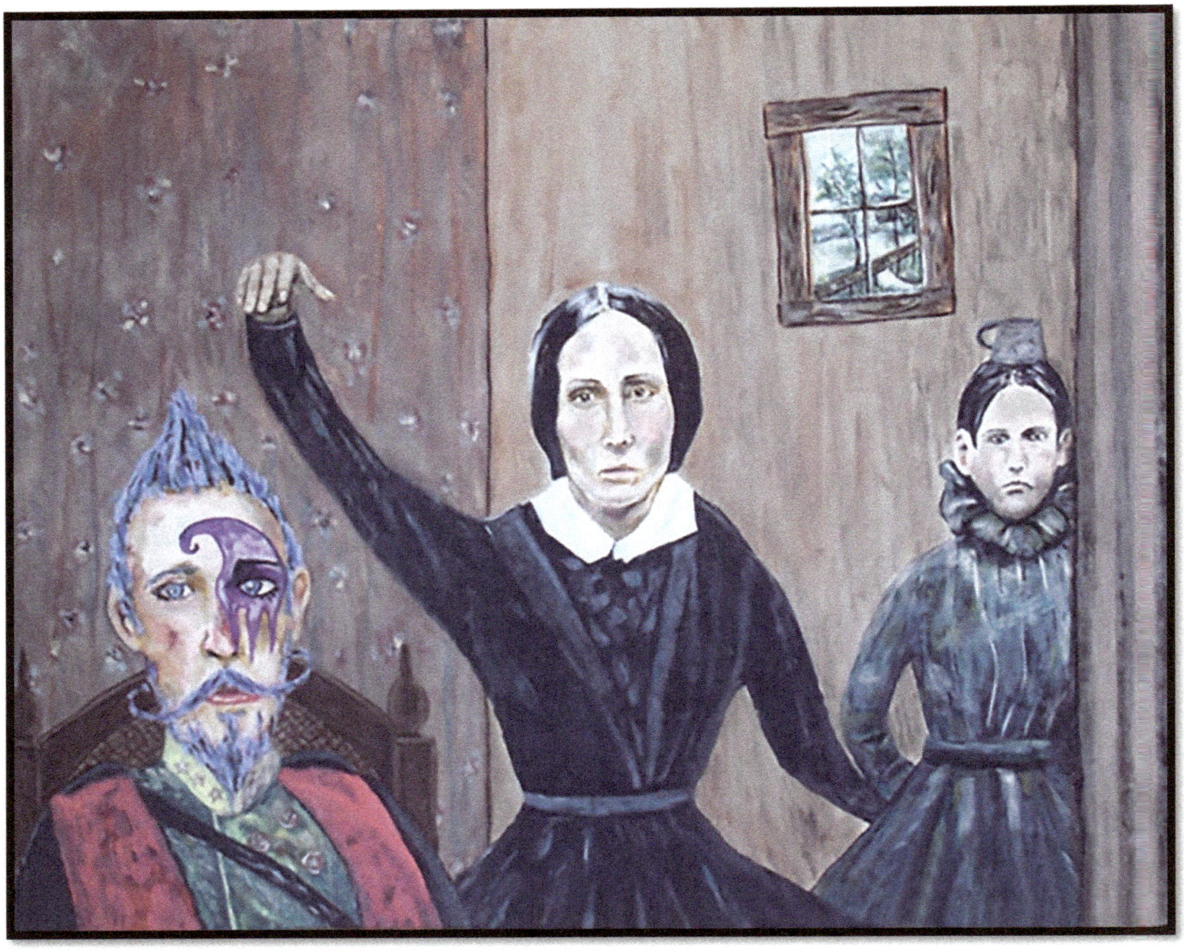

THE DEAL OF THE DAY BECAME THE TALK OF THE TOWN

The whole town began talkin'
When Martha Brown tried to barter
Her husband or her daughter
In a private auction that damn autumn.
But the only bid that went
Was for her house and her horse named Austin.
Now she spends her time walkin'
From the lawyers to her tent.

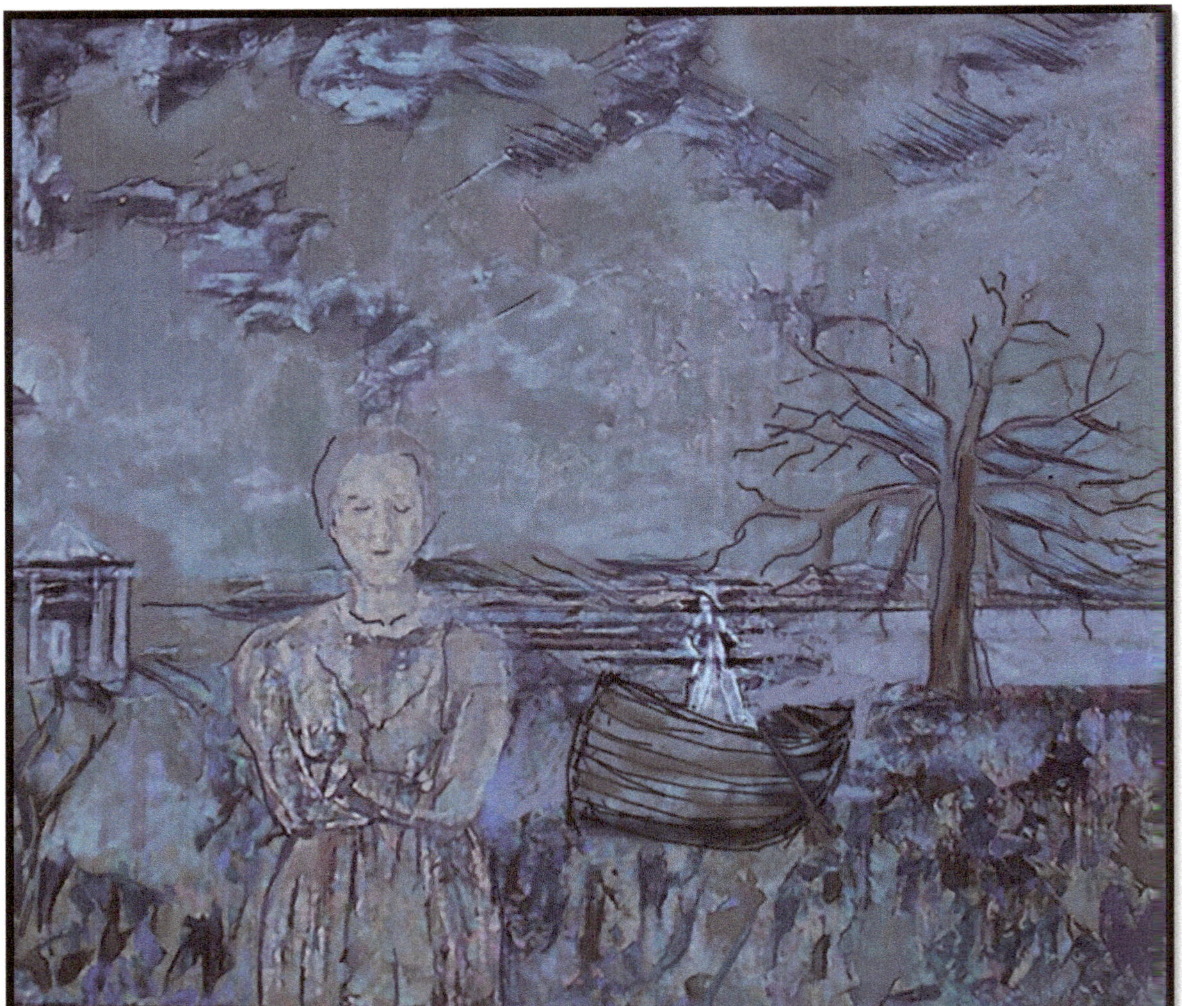

SARAMANE'S MUFFLED GRAVE

Scoop, scoop the ashes and soot
Whilst Saramane wanders and whines
All through the night, the insects they bite,
And my hands are muddy from clawing.
She takes her sweet time, drifting 'neath vines and amorphic mounds of Kudzu creeping and crawling.
Gripe, gripe, spewing her tripe.
Hurl and heave, fingers they bleed, unearthing cavernous roots.
Breaking my back when my eyes catch a crack of her
Stomping her cumbrous foot.
What I sew she rips
What's the tizzy? Tsk, tsk.
She'll be six feet beneath loose sod I heap
Tonight.
Why? Why did you lose your wits, your patience, your mind?
Hereafter, fret not: grime shall wash off your entombing trough
Like pearls rinsing from swine.

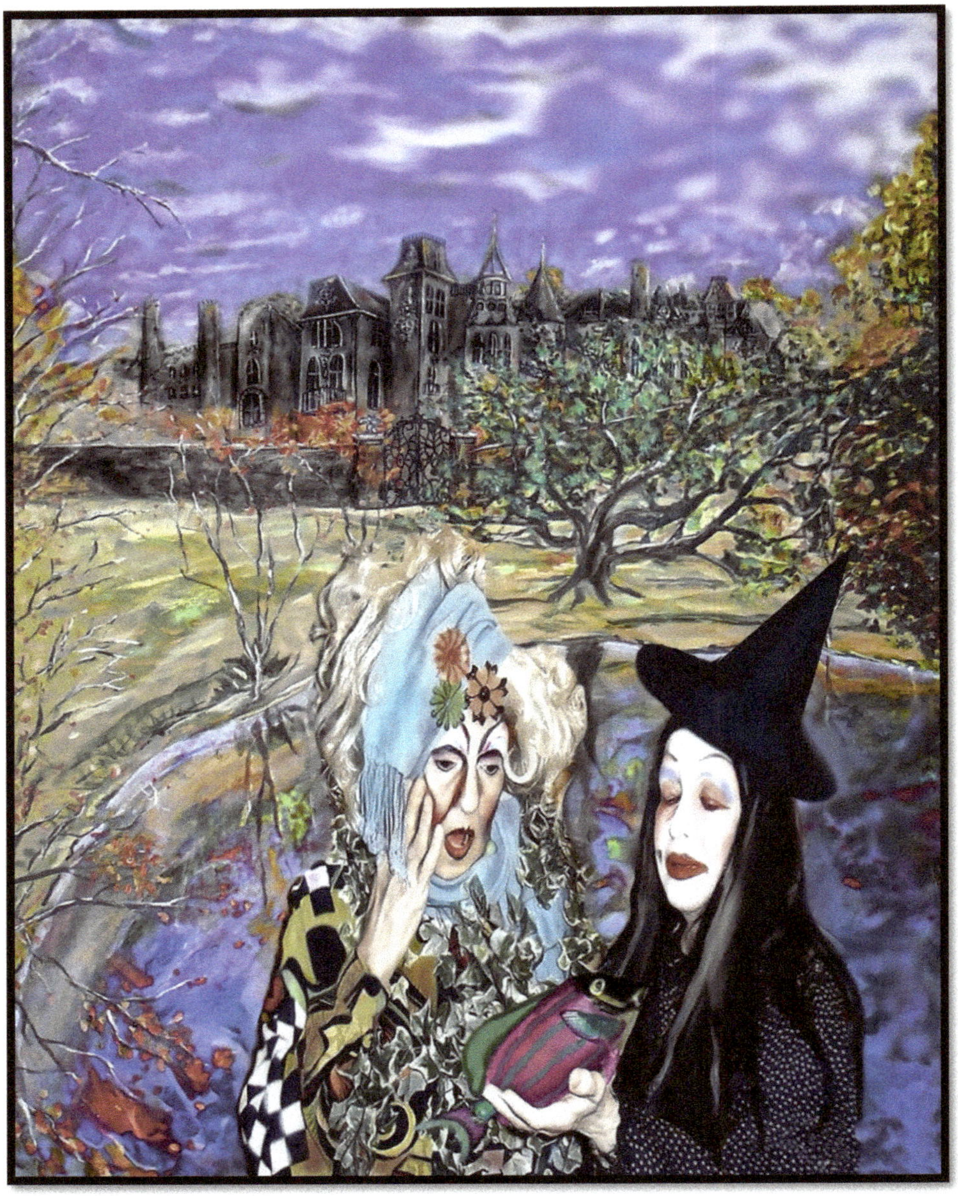

THE PROFIT FROM COLD WATERED TAILS

Having a common enemy binds friends like shallow novellas
Betwixt bookends.
The head or the tale shall not flounder to swell
Unless the boat they are rocking severs whilst fishing
On united scales.
They babble like brooks. The catch was their hook —
A whale of a minnow dinner.
The foe is the winner.
Served half-baked or mounted —
No eonic prophets from sails.

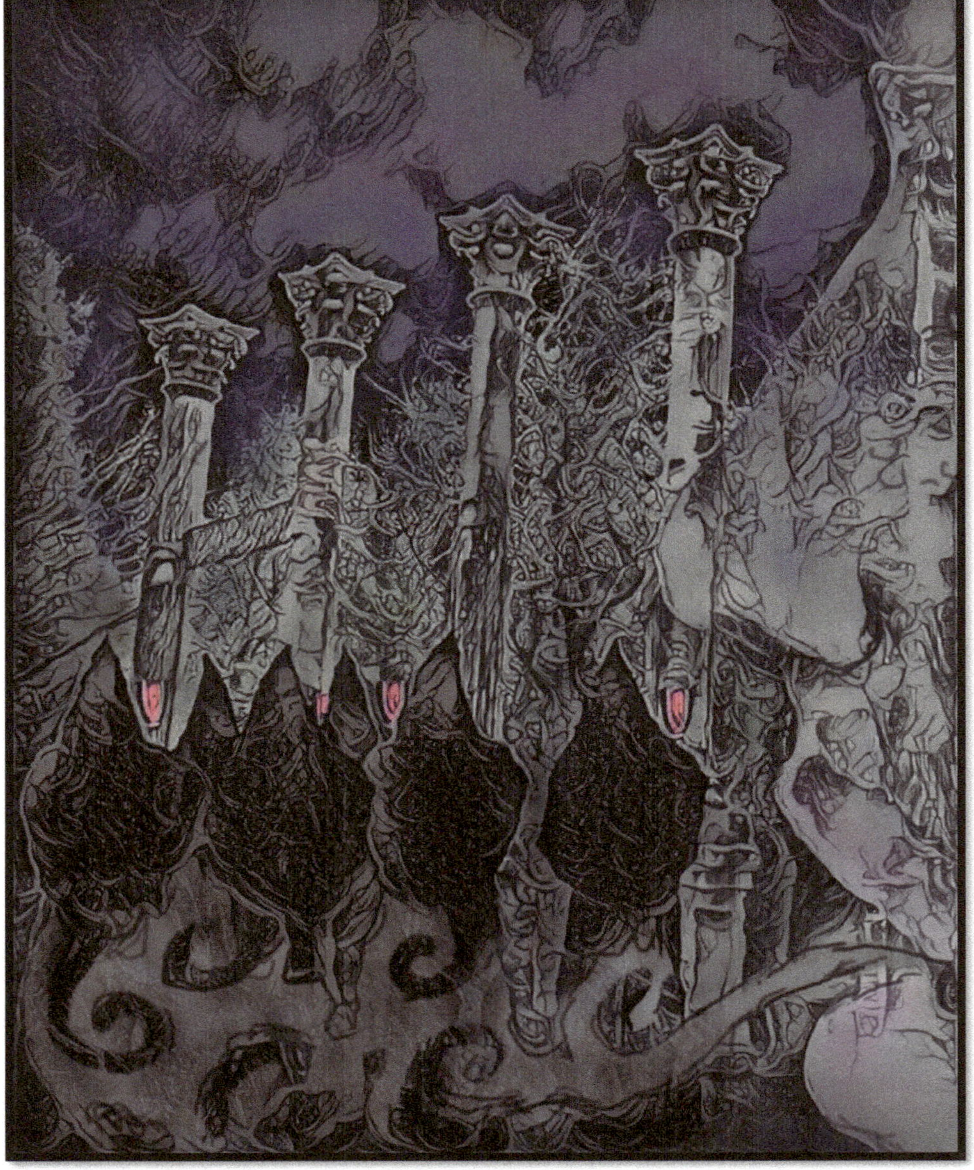

VOWEL-LADEN VERSIFIERS

Deep in the sanguine lair of wanton lads and vamps so fair,
They raise a flute of the finest of verve's stored rubescent portion.
Silken oooo's, voluptuous vowels, make ruin
While hand-locked prudes brood beyond the runes that stand still,
Their flower-cuffed, waxen hands attain
Only the hems of tie-died myths.
While S's and Aints wane yet remain in wind x'd panes,
Sibylline syllables committing literary death,
It could never contain their consonant breath.

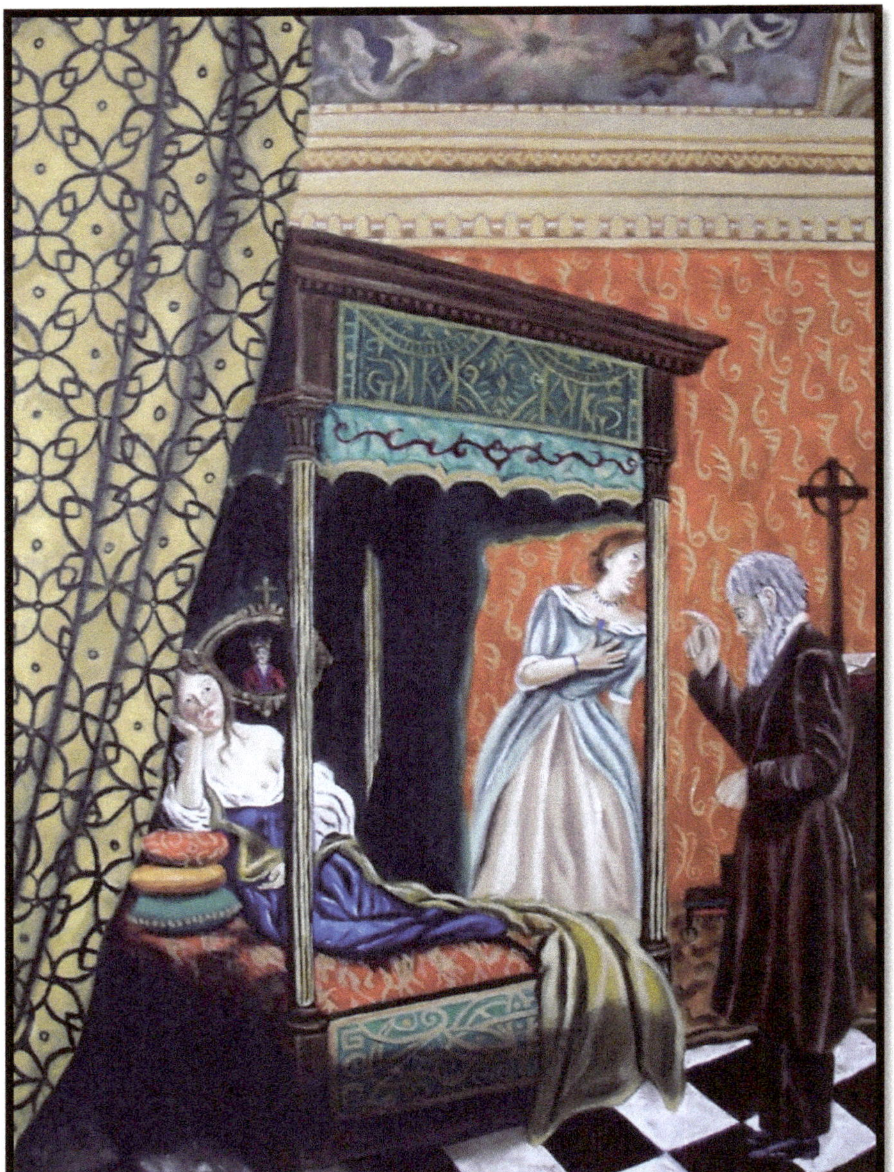

ROAMING IN THE GLOAMING

Stalking under rooftop blankets in the gloaming,
Eyeing evangelists belching bacon.
Revelation:
Science, order must pursue
Not command papal paper and glue.
Cloister for one and sell for more.
Anti-waves against anti-shore.
Greeted by reason, they slam the door,
Building bandaged armies awaiting white horses.
Antibiotics, more.
Stepping-stones spilling the blood that gives them strength.
The truth, abhor.

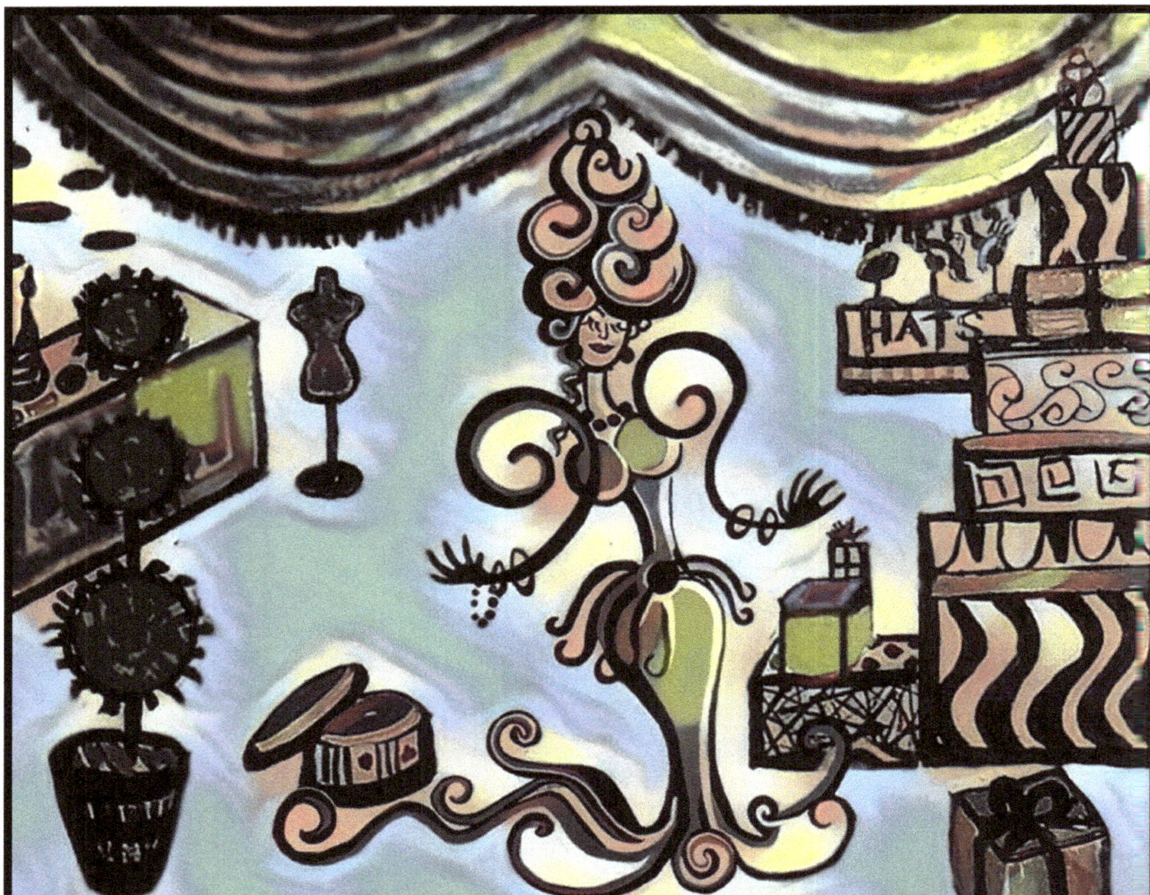
HATS

WHAT DRIVES ME CRAZY?

It's there, not here, that matters in society, even when they rush eternity.
"You must work me in for a day of beauty. Yes, I know it's so sudden.
But, hey — it's me!
I'm going out of town, you see.
Where no one will know or remember me.
Matters more than the here and now reality.
I can't deal with it because I'm going out of town in the morning.
Making you think I'll be performing brain surgery.
Or accept an award for my integrity.
When in all honesty, there was an outlet sale in Desolate Springs —
A big sale on skinny jeans
And books on time managing.
Sorry, I never got your message on my answering machine,"
she said, slurping from a plastic cup of tea.
"You'll have to reschedule me. I'm busy in the justifiable region for passive-aggressive lackadaisy.
If but a mere five miles from my normal vicinity,
'out of town' counts—technically,
When no one can actually see."

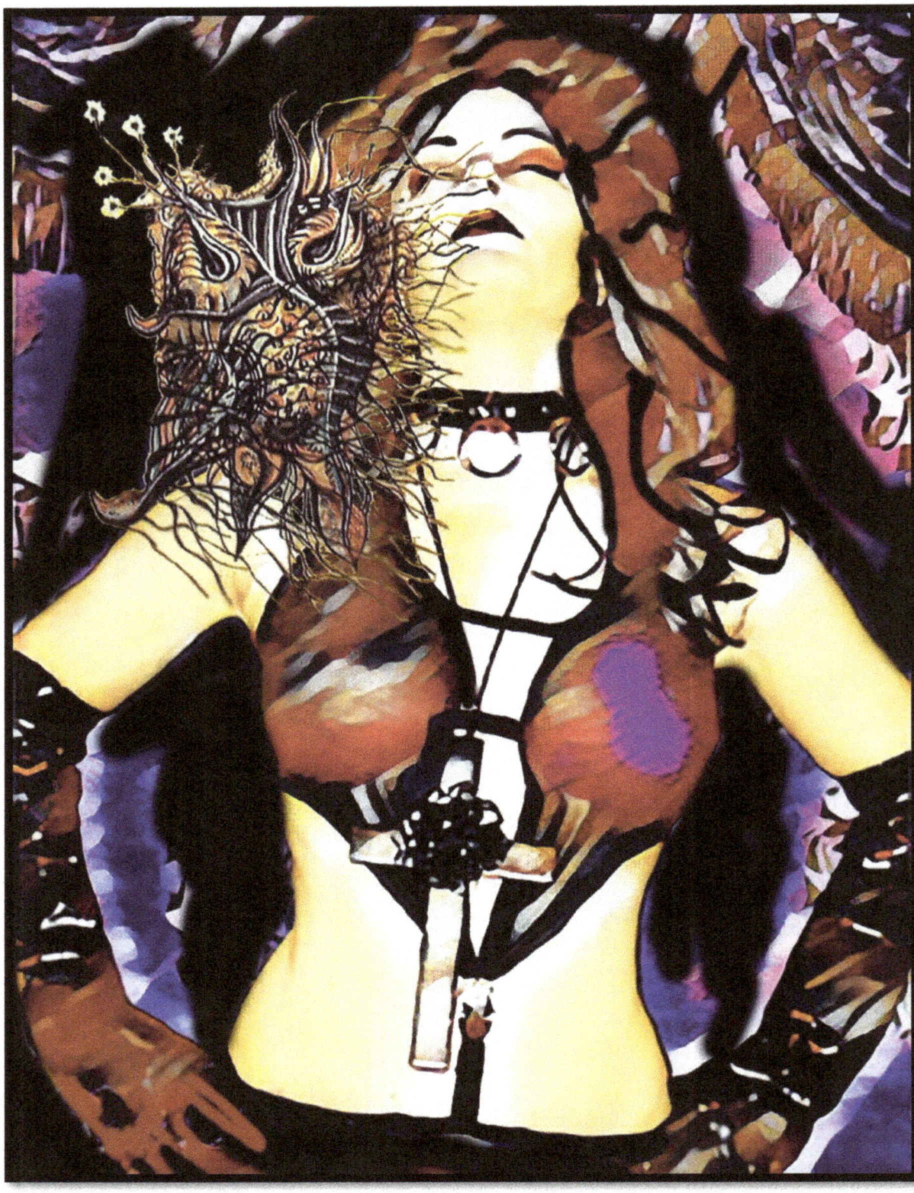

WHICH WITCH'S WISH?

That which is beautiful to me: a jinxed widow
Peeking 'neath the wreathed window o'er the snowy streets below.
'Tain't a which but a witch asleep, discreet and mellow,
Breathing slow, dreaming of singing willows and weeping cellos.
She foresees the sweet owl on her pillow.
With feathers on its feet a-billow,
'Twas not an owl but armadillo,
And it doesn't give a hoot, you know,
But a "who" through its beak oh so yellow.
And as her crow, with legs of three, grows mold on its toes,
She released it from her dreams
Like familiars and totems of old.
Lo and behold, her armadillo leaned low,
And out the window, it bellowed,
"Keep free of deceit, golden-winged fellow."

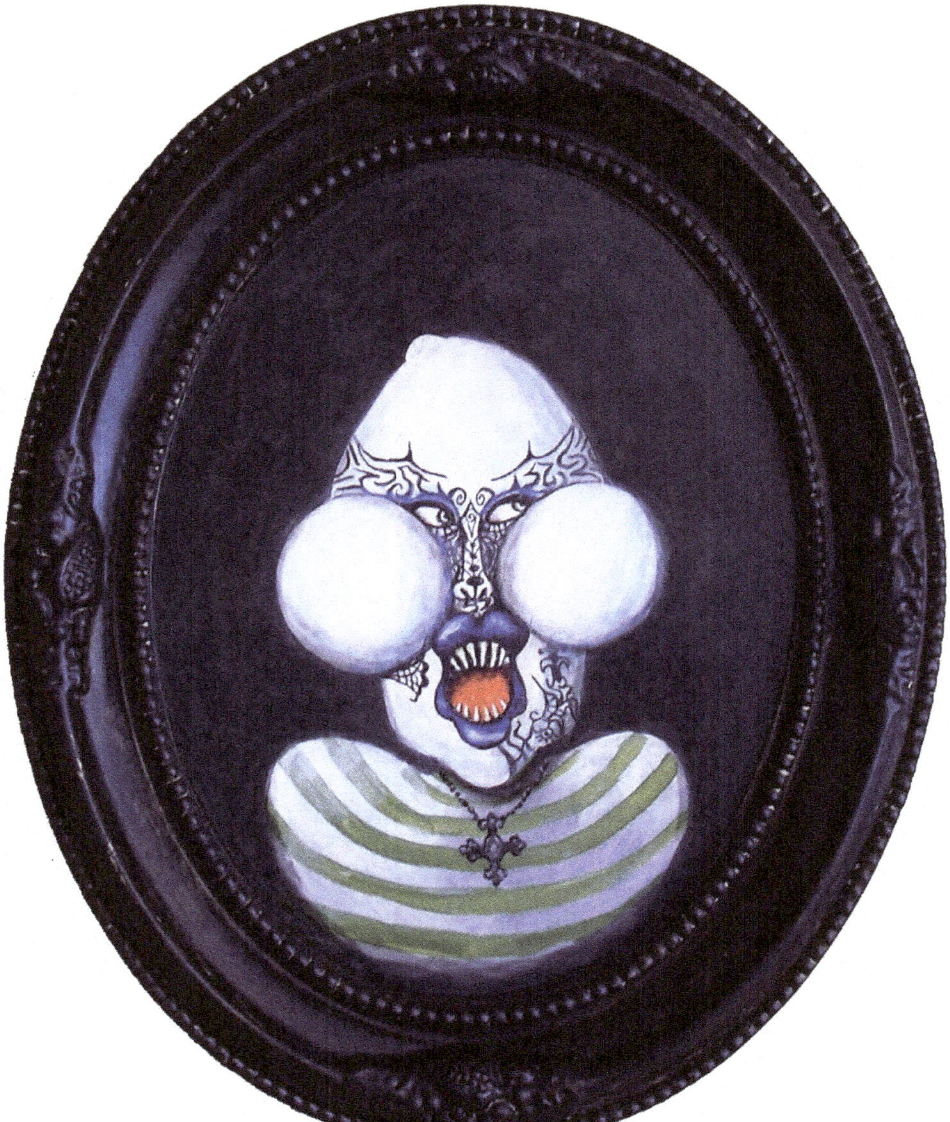

GULPINPLUMP

With ether for lunch, Gulpinplump gets a bit cheeky.
I have a hunch he misses meals weekly.
Hanging in frames and munching on wheezes.
Collecting, on his teeth, residual breezes.

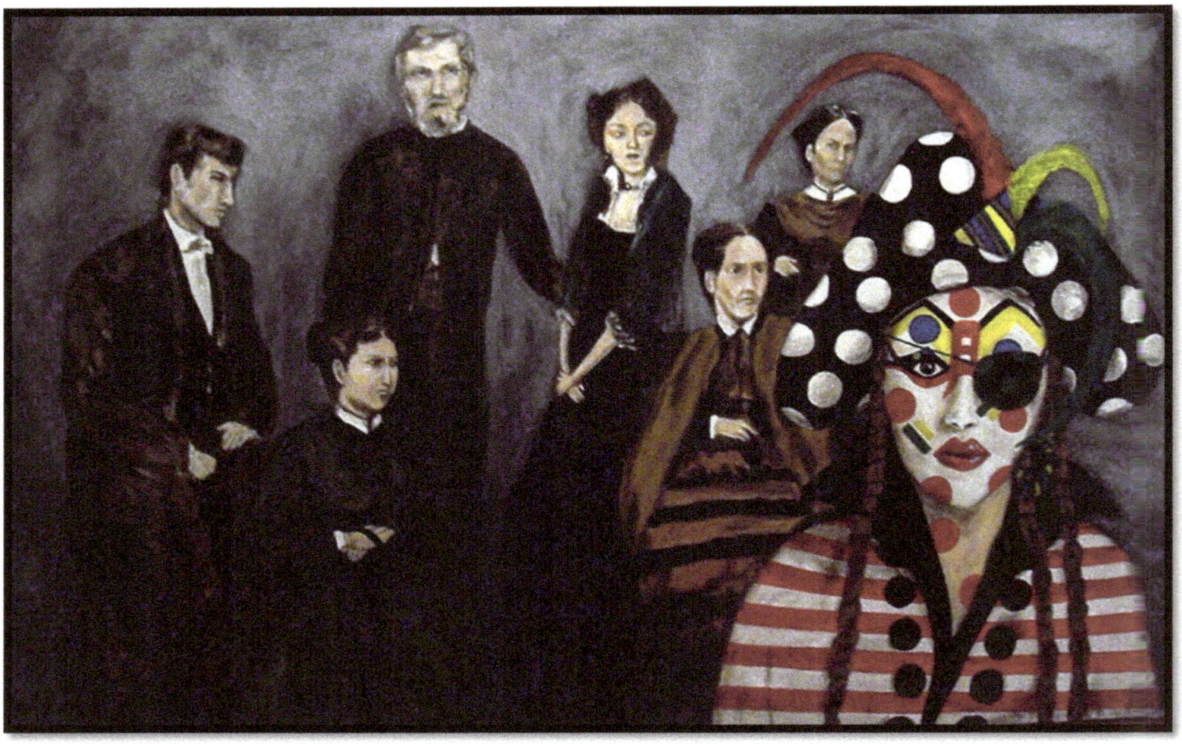

SOME BESTS ARE KEPT SECRET

Does it still work
To throw a fit alone?
You've got nobody, and you've got no home.
You lost your money, but you still have worth.
An award sits crammed in your baggage,
Recognizing not the things you have said
But the years you held your tongue —
Bit your lips at what the world has done.
"A rare gem under the earth."
So, it has been said,
Behind iron curtains,
In front of an audience so deaf.
This, surely, is a lifetime test.

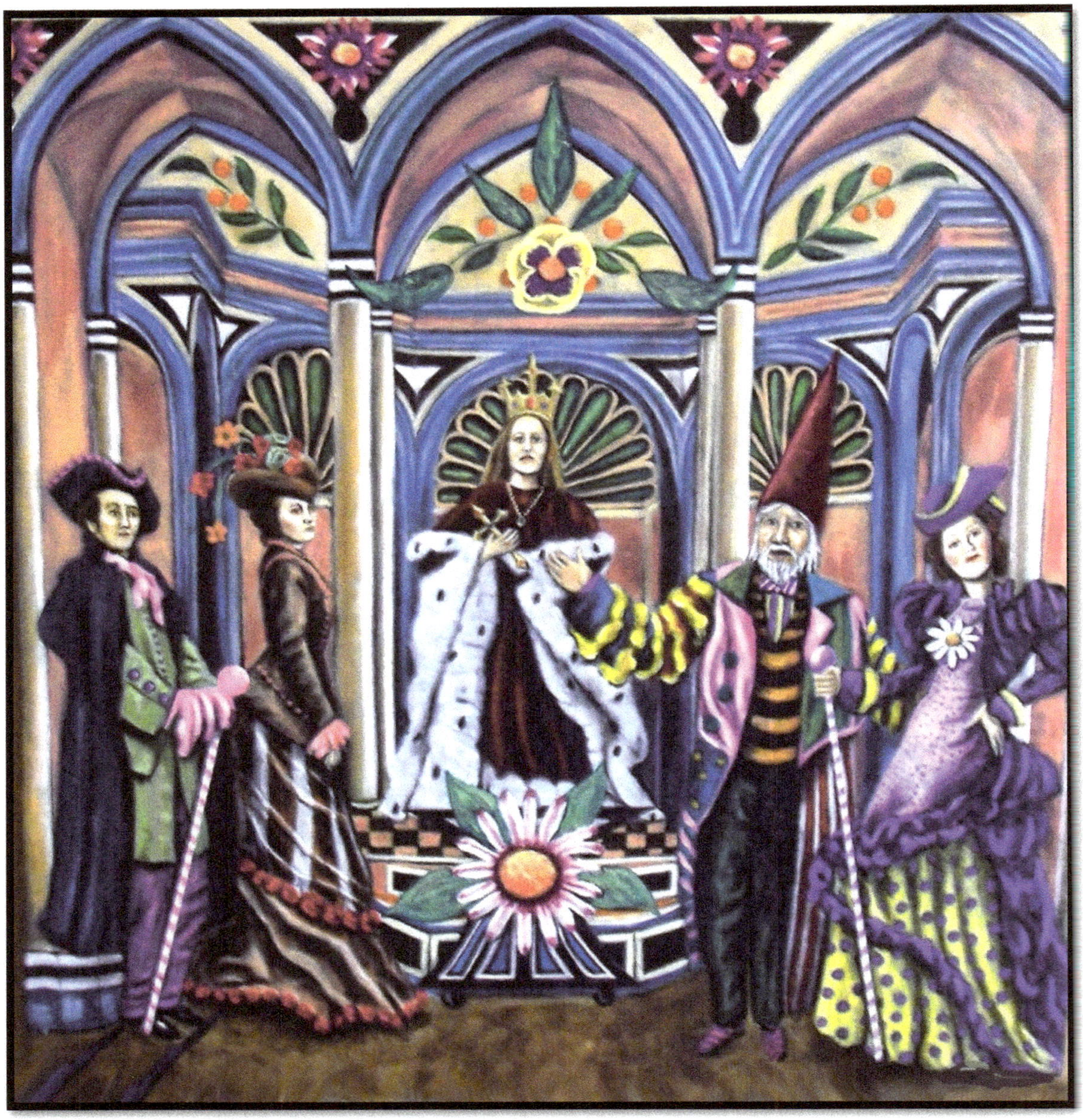

BASEMENT RADICALS CRASHING MY SABBATICAL

Costumed crusaders recruiting invaders
Will house their tanks in your palace,
Keeping their homes neutral as dry bones,
Private and secluded — hypocrisy eluded —
Expecting my platform to serve as a sounding board.
What use is your feuding fashion
Without a dash of that passion at your masked bastion?
It's like a layered cake —
A month late. Unbalanced. Half baked.

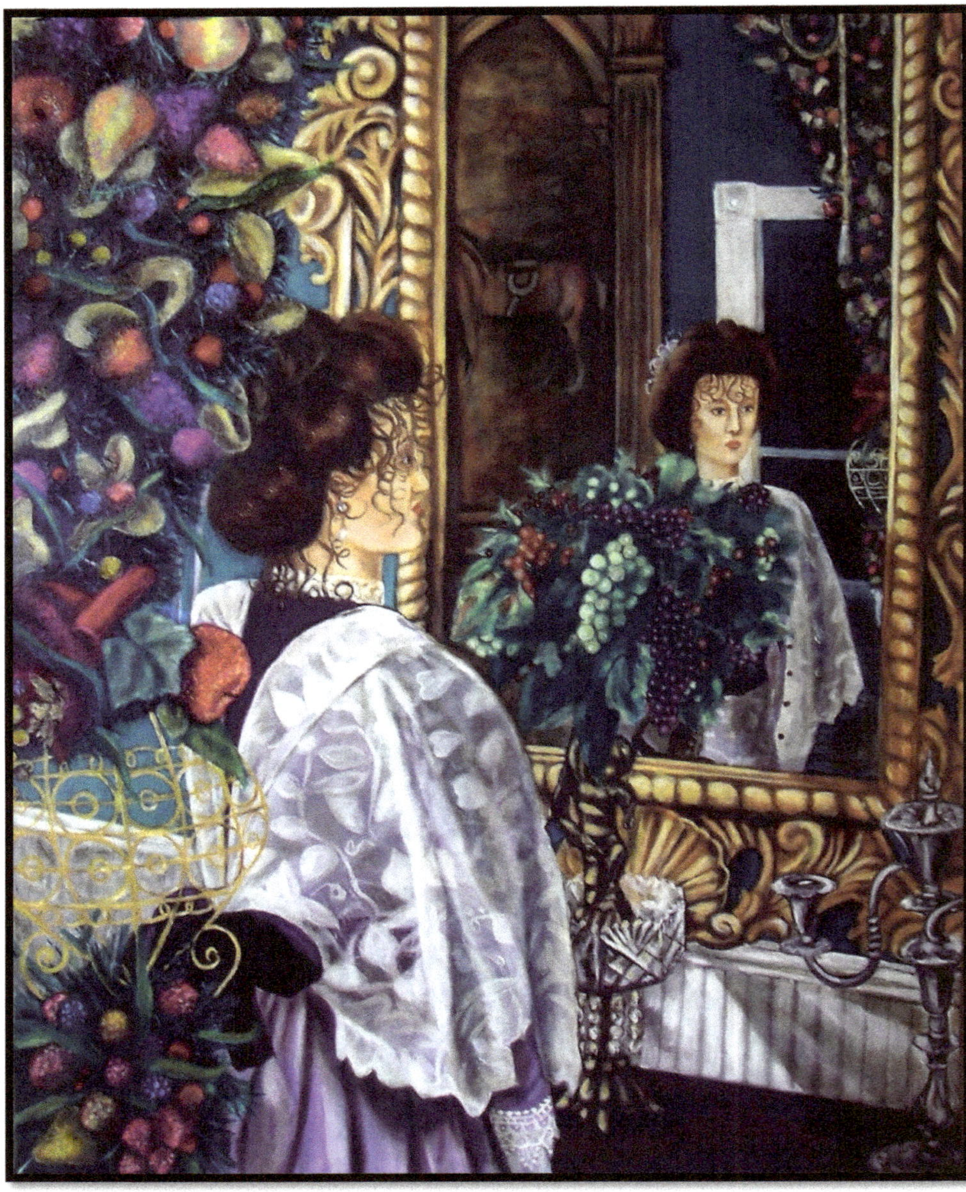

SHEDDING TEARS WITH THE SHELLEYS

Deep inside my ignorant soul
Is an articulation,
A literary celebration,
Transforming my tortured past
Into a romantic
Encapsulation.
But will they swallow
The artist's purge,
The community scourge,
Before death soon follows
The printed maturation?

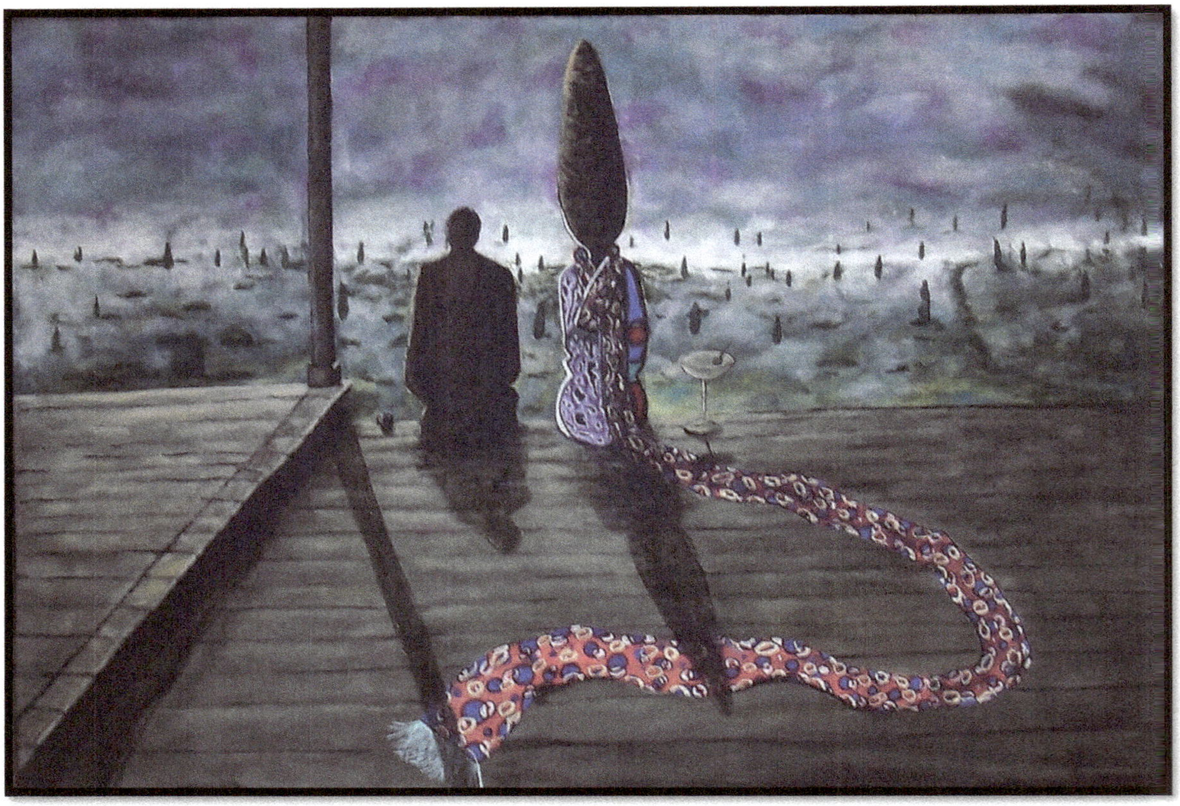

UNPREDICTABLE AUDIENCE

Yin and yang in reverse.
Fashion-forward and rehearsed.
Without apologies, they step to the beat,
Sleek repeat,
Hoping others have heard worse,
And that they were the victors,
For their souls were delivered
Without a flinch or note to quiver.
And that might just be
The only condition that set them free.

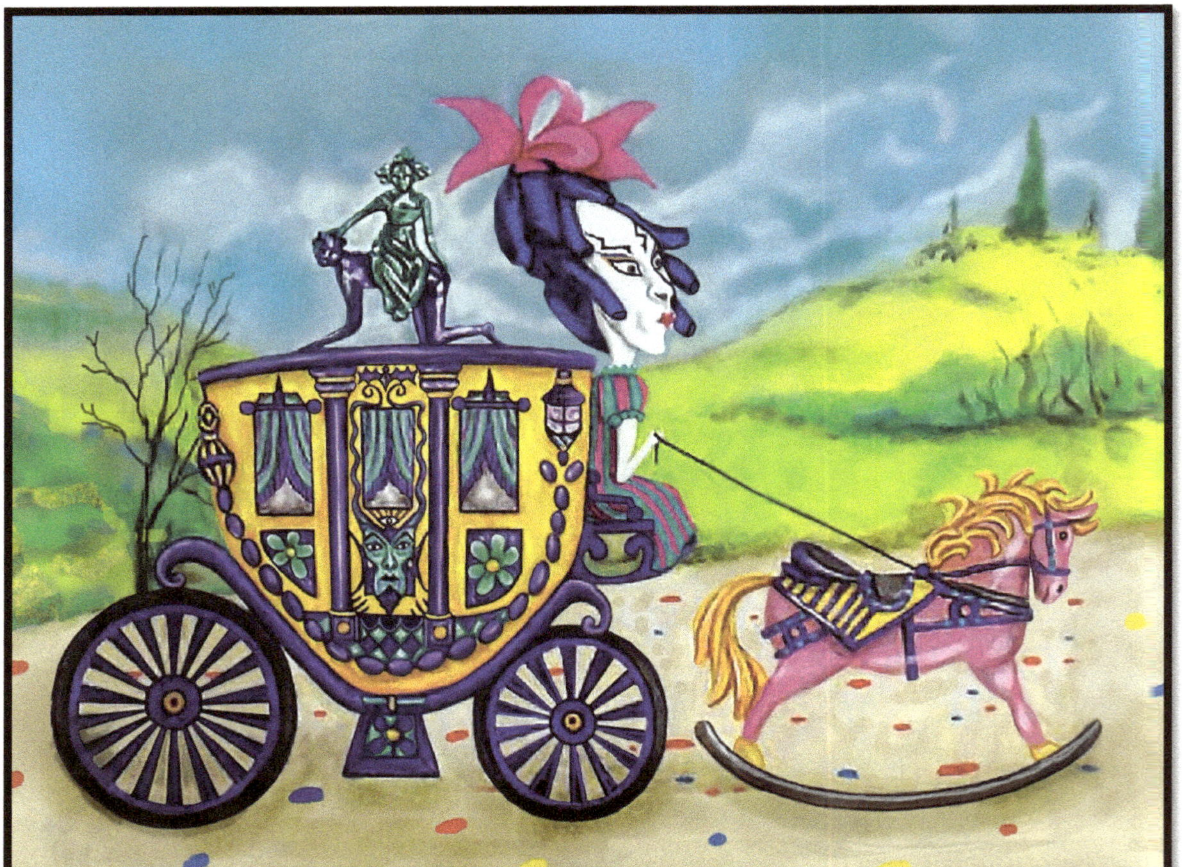

PATTY'S WAGON

Perfectly private Patty plopped atop her wagon
And ordered her rocking horse "home!"
But her smile wilted like cabbage,
Hearing the knocking in the carriage.
No, she was not traveling alone.

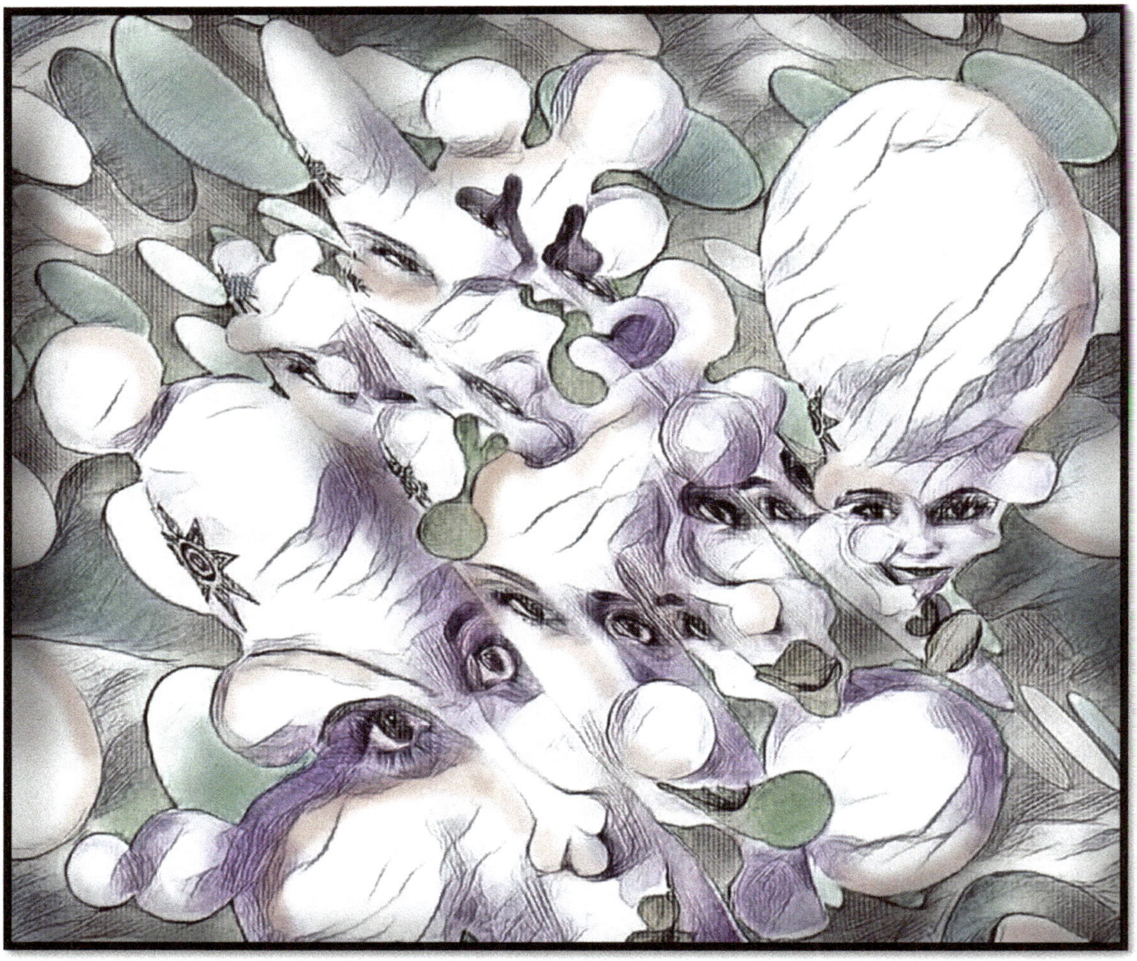

UNIFACIAL RESPACEMENT

Planets are a waste of space.
We should replace barren balls of dust with ever-morphing faces,
Flesh and blood expressions,
Peering, peeping on the human race with astronomical obsession.

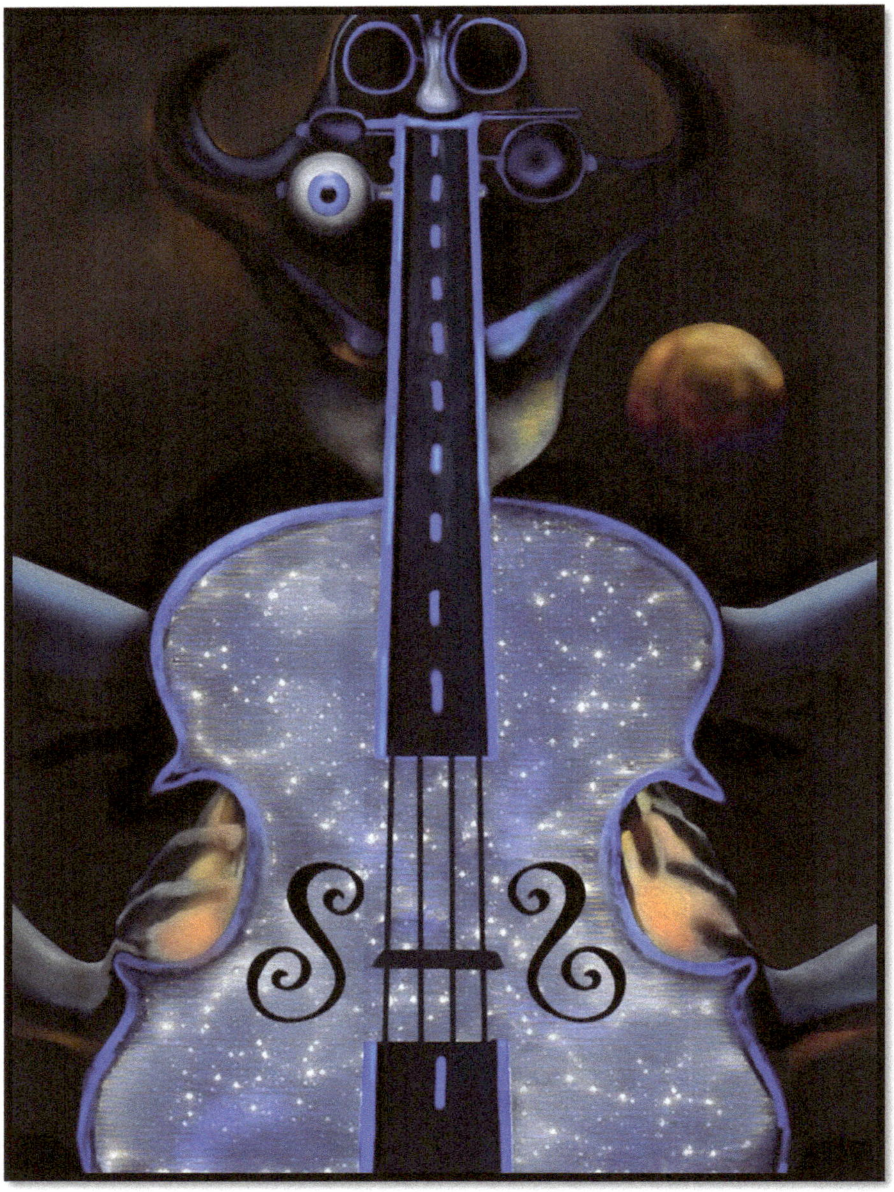

NO TASTO IN RELATIVE MINOR

This sawing of gut strung on wood is hot,
Gurgling supreme when it sings.
Long neck,
Faux purfling not.
Stop fiddling and listen to it row.
Danse macabre before they stop and rosin the bow.

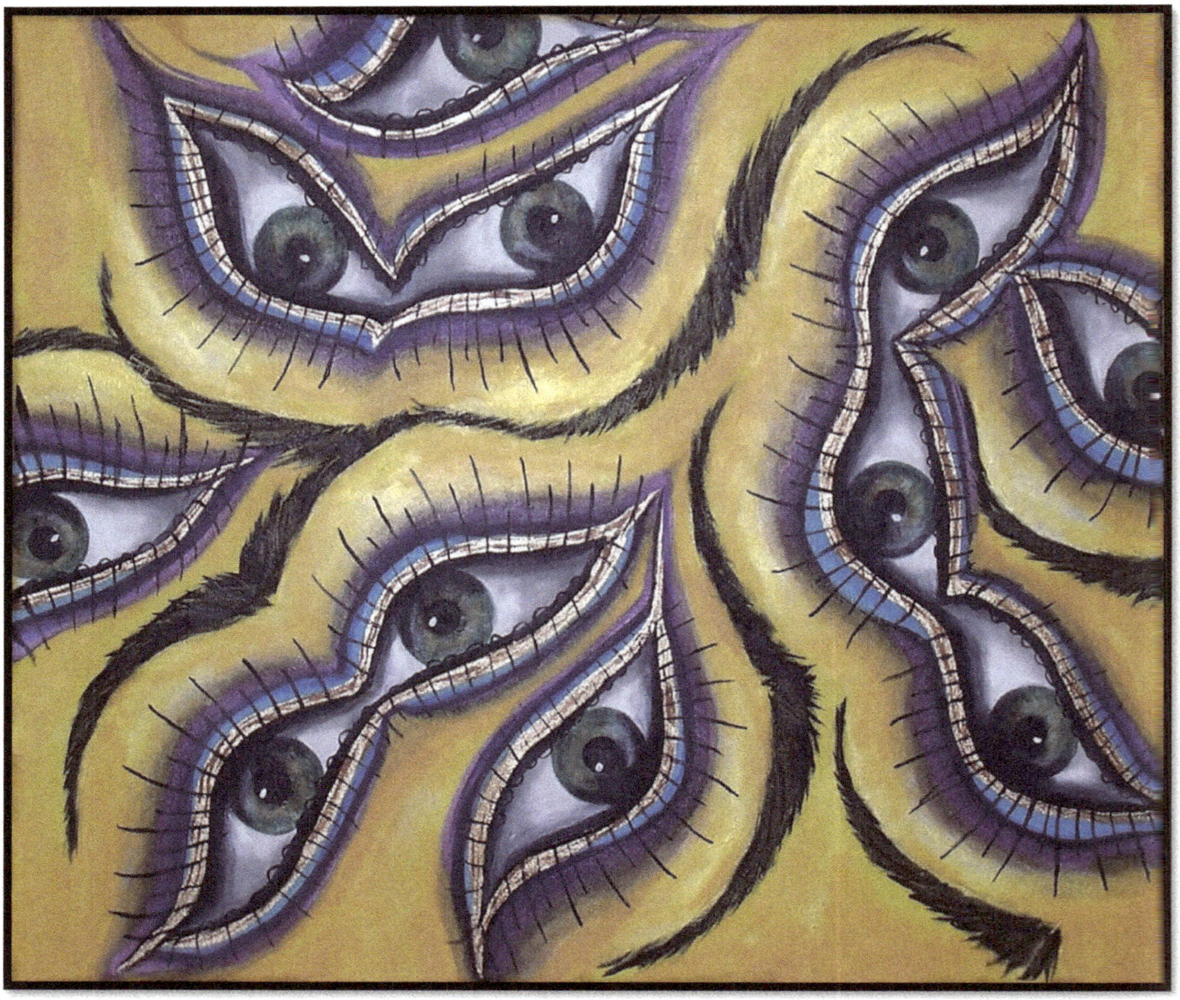

ANATOMY APPROPRIATION

What Your Eyes See When You Don't Perceive
(Never Sleep When Reading)

Tattooed leaves upon eyelid sleeves.
Quilled embraces barbed in blood and in word
Composes "a dirge for the skilled," the spine fluid said,
As it danced for the blinded and read for the dead.
The pimpled plates of leathery fate
Took its revelations o'er tailbone and face.
Contoured traces.
Coal-black laces.
Crisscross brows from vows and warm, naughty places.

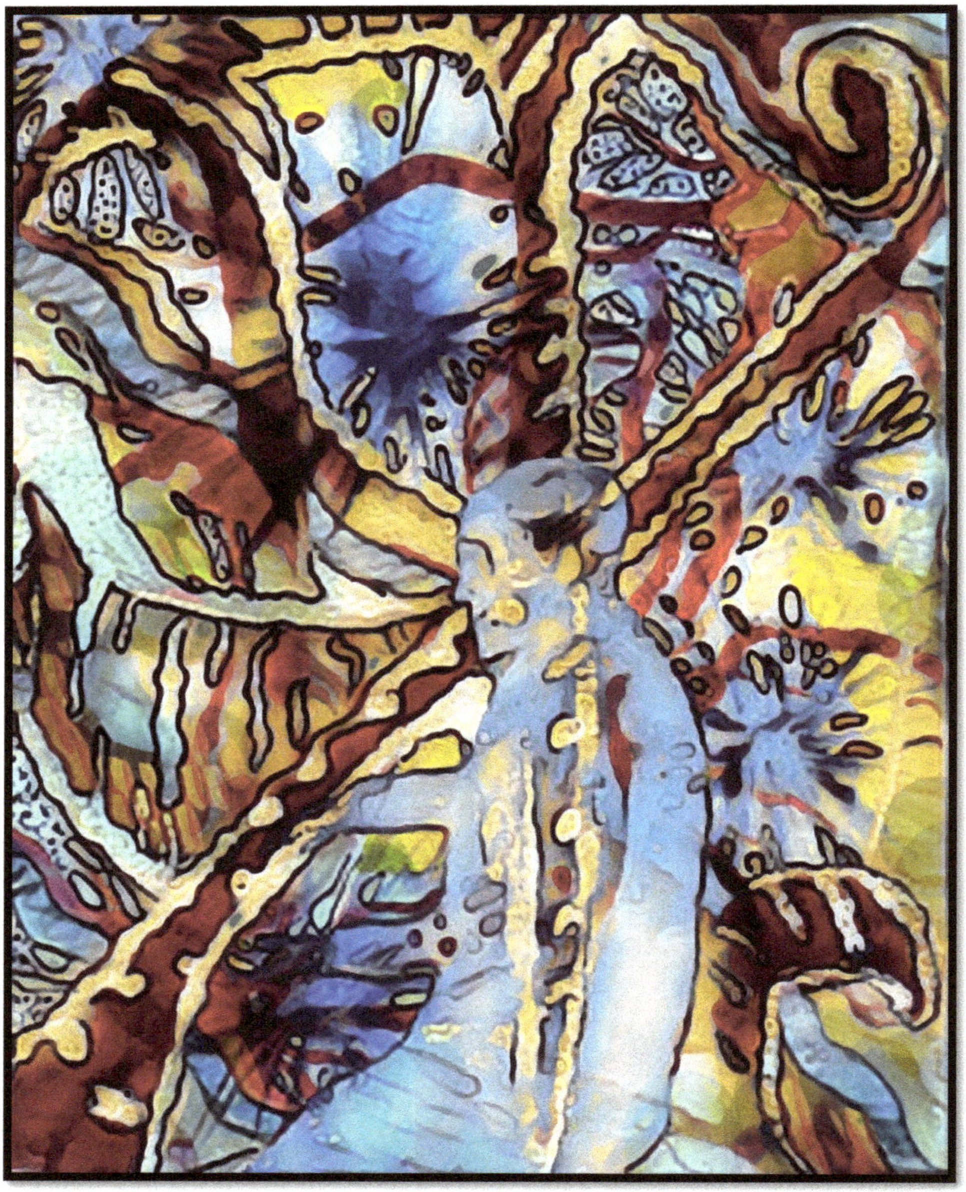

SKULLDROPS

Skulldrops falling on my head.
Heaven's tears dropping death.
Dying's not for me.
I have crossed over,
Bypassed the grave,
The crimson,
The clover.

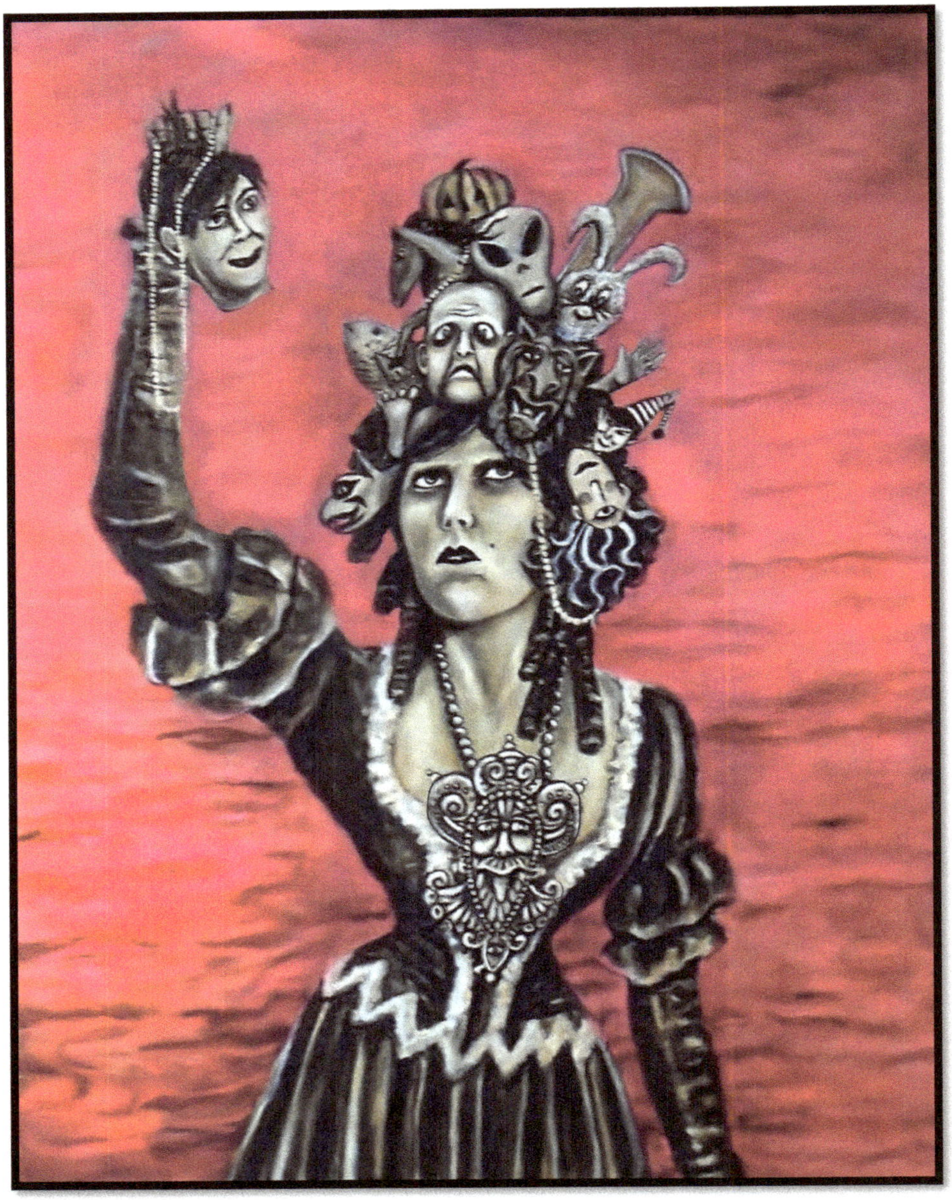

ODE TO GENOLA

Lost fragments floating upon alleys now rivers of blood,
The City of Severance,
The lost love.
Genola's dreams washed away.
Perhaps they will drift ashore
Some day.
Her spirit still wanders,
Her sorrow floats.
Mortals do not see her,
Her projection of hope.
She still drowns her sorrows,
Still wades past boats,
Collecting trinkets and beads
And unholy ghosts.

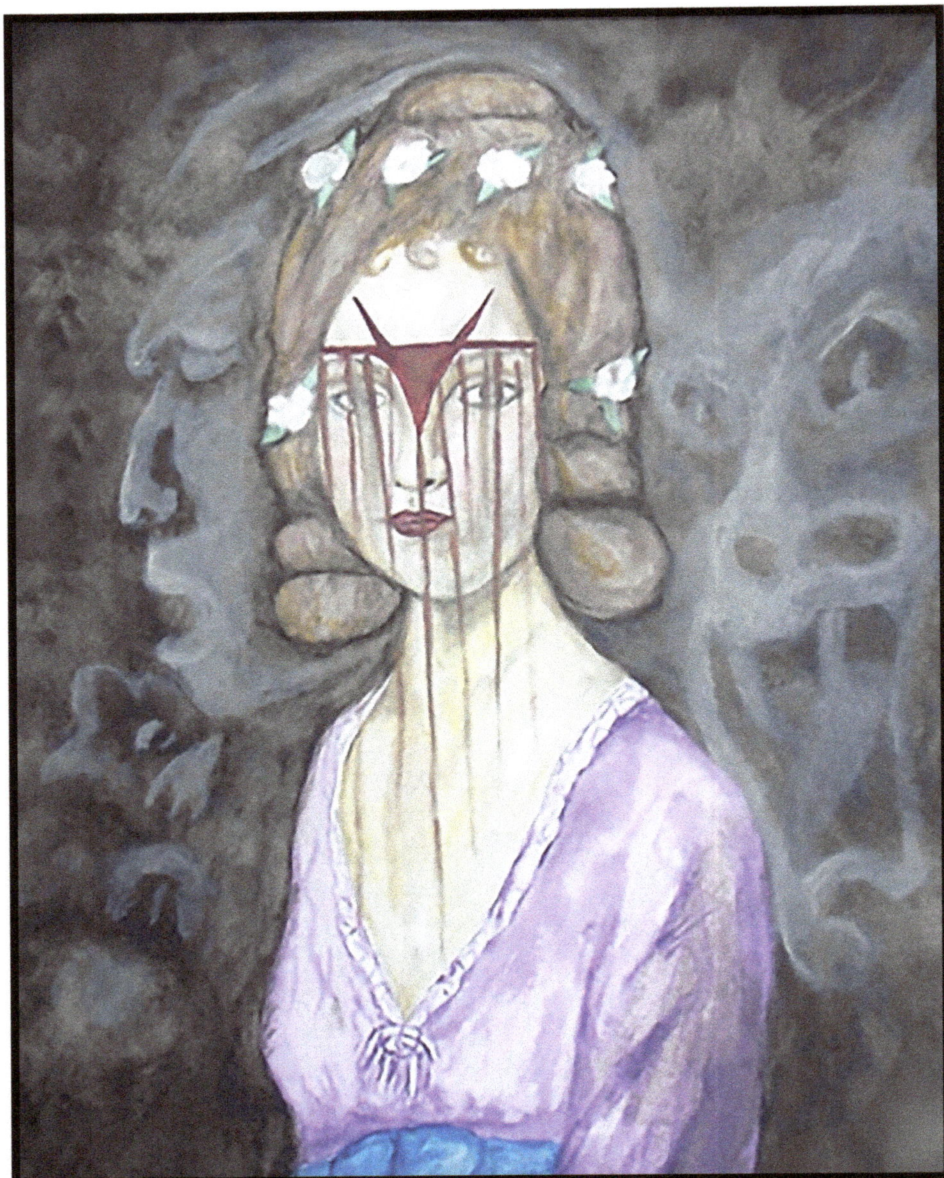

JUGULAR JONGLEUR

V^^V

The paradoxes of the pure are vagabondly virtuous,
Clinically voluptuous.
Their "worthlessness" you lure into padded alleys
Darkened with pinstriped plans and poke-veined pain
To which they joyously feign.
Your epithet should read, "Here We Lie Gratified from the Bounty of All
Who Bleed."

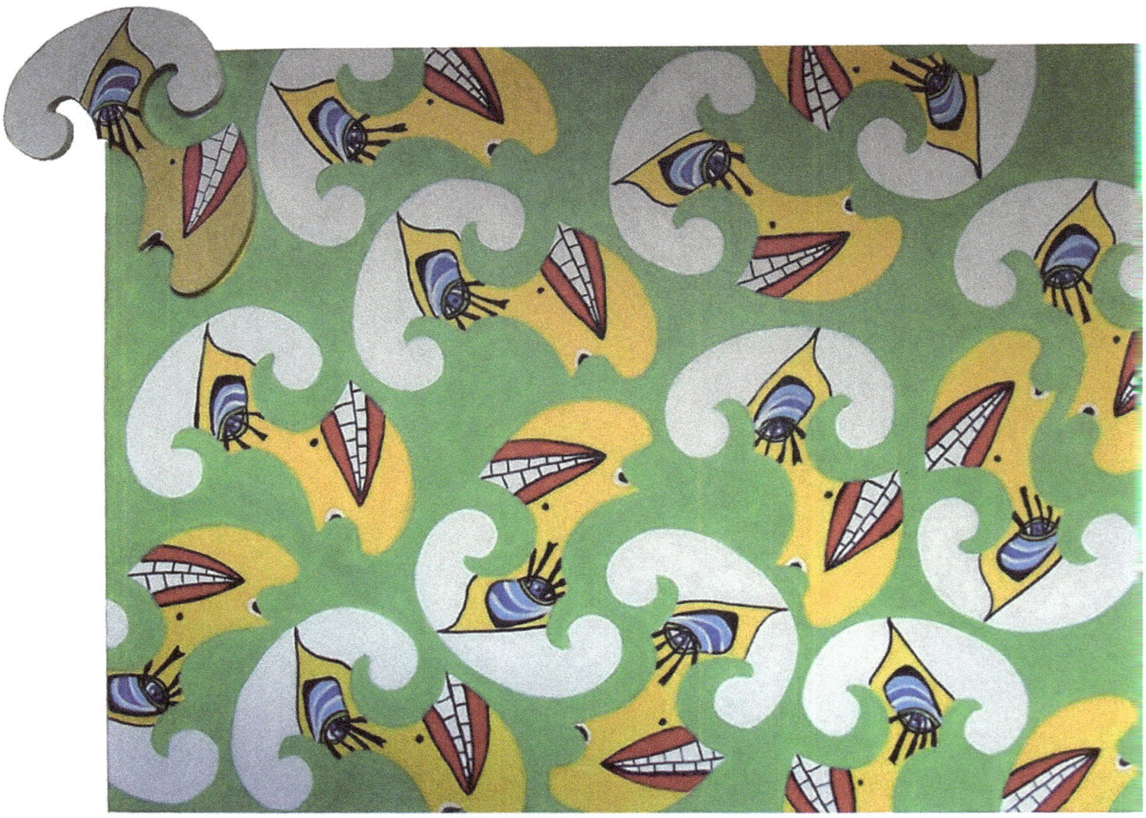

TWEET DEFEAT

You know your peeps were just being sweet
When your two-bit tweet becomes obsolete
Behind a blitz of meat pics on a plate
Some VIP ate.
And the only likes you get for the day
Are in a thread of GIFs to a friend
Nowhere near your vacant page.

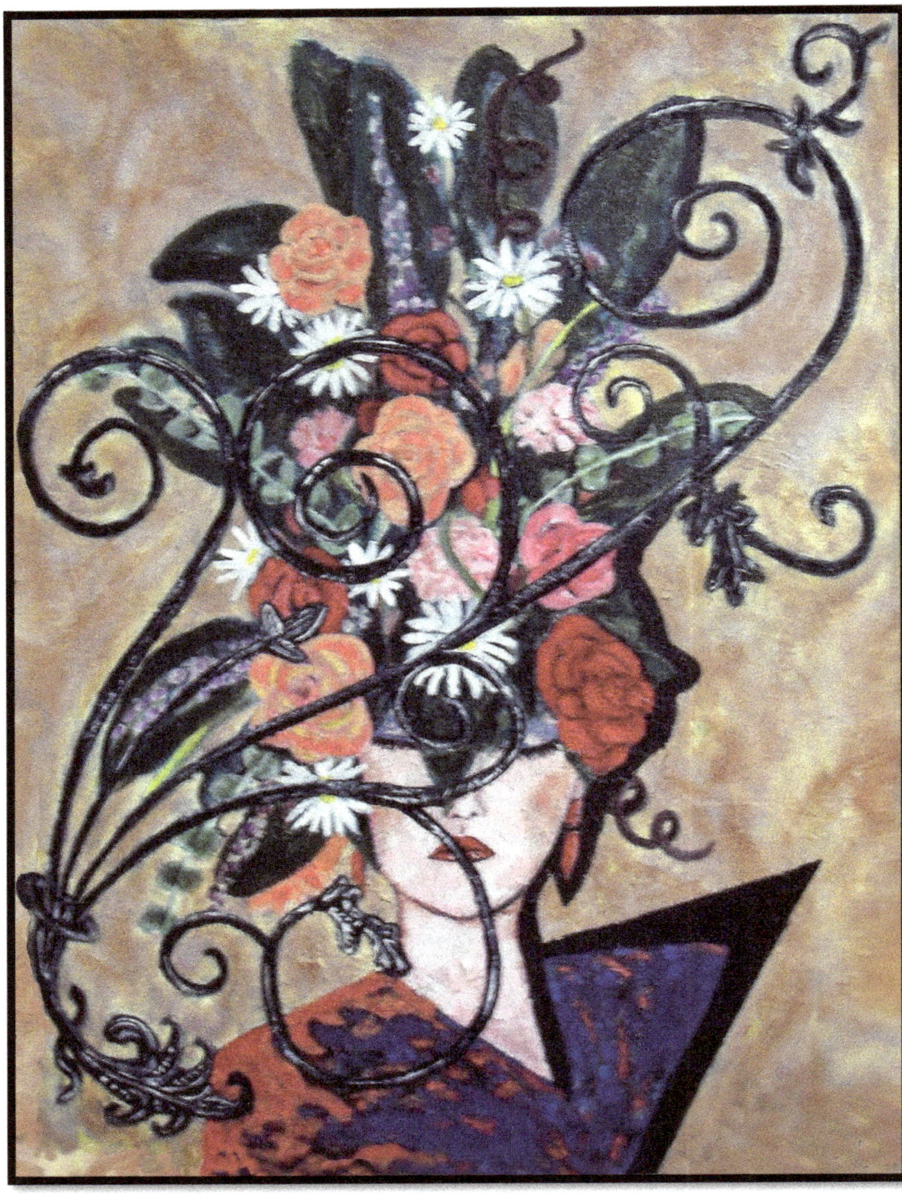

SOCIAL FORUM POEM

Here are pics of my puppies' and kittens' pink fuzzy mittens.
I'm having a blessed day on vacay, making family confections,
Using my new convection oven in my sunlit kitchen.
I nearly forgot to mention after I got home from confession:
Sugar took her first steps at Grannie's third wedding!
Yes, in her ribbons, ringlets, and little lacy leggings.
But I pray you take this with my sincerest intention,
Since you ignored my farm request and candy crushing perfection:
Bobby hit a home run at Little League and
Got all A's on his lessons.
He's going to make America great again, and be a real blessing,
As soon as he figures out which decade is worthy of duplication.

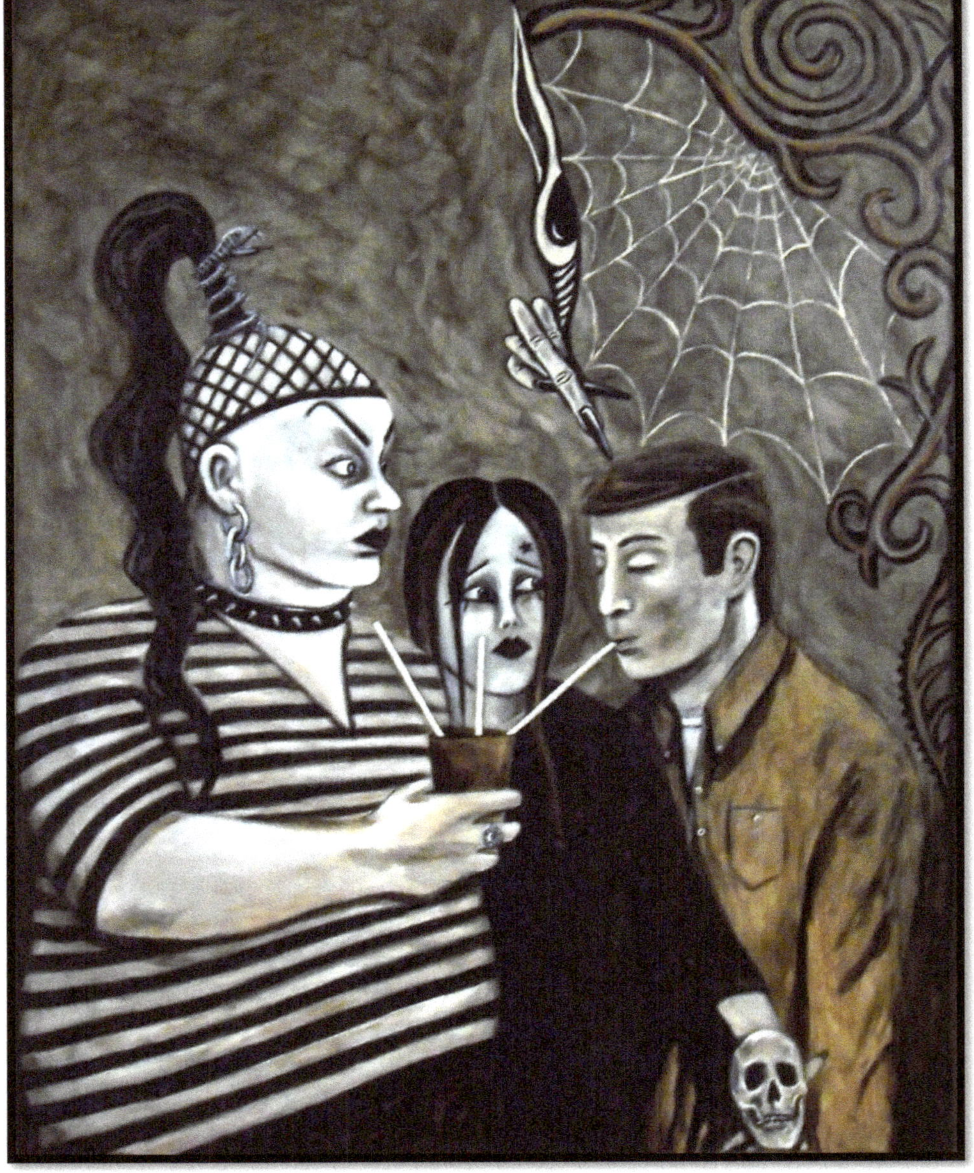

LEECHES

My afterglow of wishful bliss
Was phantom reality converging in the mist,
Drifting o'er loins and knotting hips,
O'er forget-me-nots and catnips.
Ships, passing, skip over oceanic foam.
Soft sheets of my memoir like syncopated stones.
I have long grown alone, in cold ears bemoaned
Leeches feasting on my song.
Depraved waves that tip the bow,
Seizing my here and now,
My only home.

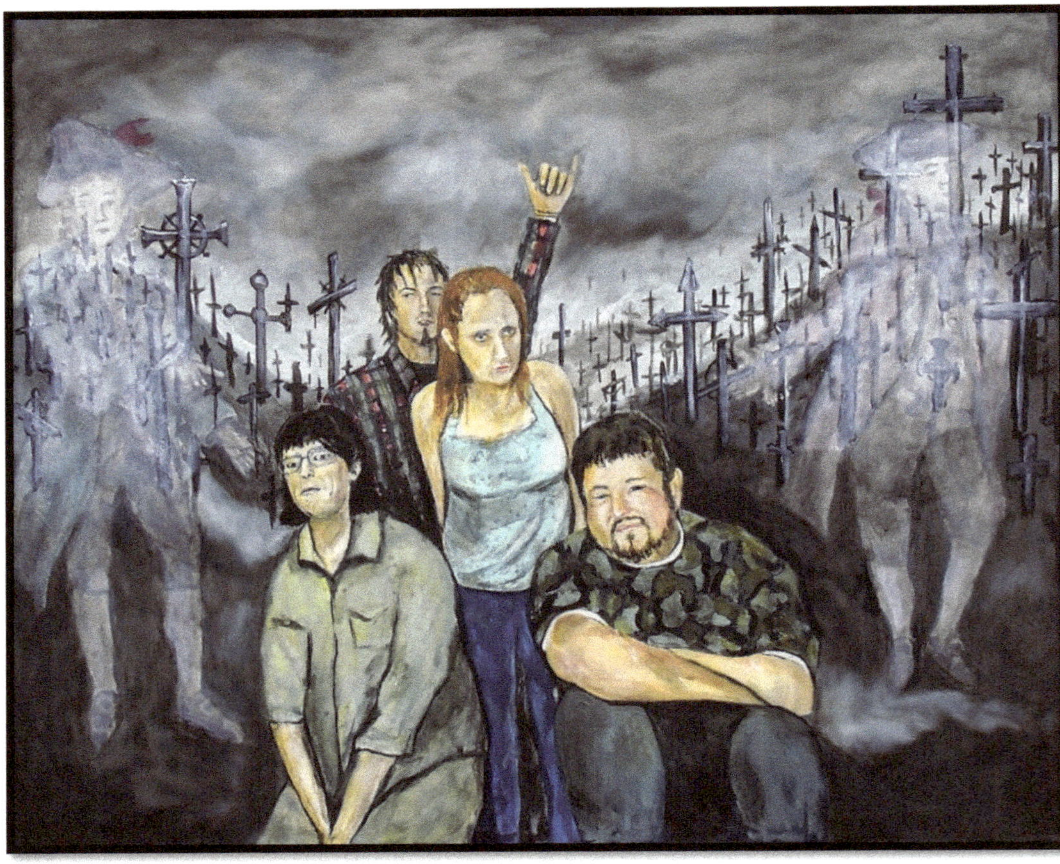

THE IMPORTANCE OF POSITIVITY IS A PESSIMIST'S LAW DEGREE

Diederik raged — and revealed, soon, his icy face.
Proud, fronting the funeral procession in place.
Even the stage attained the malaise of his feet.
Oh, yes, the graves sealed upon seeing his hate.
They trembled so — gasped low — for no lips were theirs to be bit.
While alertly stilled, the anxious guests reminisced.

A mute of mayhem evaporated from earth's putrid pits,
Which the blah-blah bourgeois, such as Diederik, dismiss
As "the verdict of spirits."
"Theirs is a cage of deception: Discretion we must applaud —
The great void — from which no ghost should ever dare crawl.
There the unnatural they whisper, planting dreadful ideas,
Stealing angelic auras from our virginal years!"
When, to no effect, from lakes of fire,
The timed plot of death is counting the hours
To lose what is theirs and take what is ours.
What freedom in cages, employing precise gages,
Damnation creeps,
Whilst fettered behind molten gates that reach to our streets.
Beats, where select love is favored and all others rejected.
Dominion opinions of erasers as party favors.
"Disgrace! My people, my race, my chosen faith," said Diederik,
With a reddened face.
"Why must you cry of this dead man's life with applied praise?
In days of old, we bit not out tongues
The sprites of lies from the other side hath made ye numb."
To this, the grieving widow could not abide:
"Listen here, old man of hate!
This graveyard, which you have defaced with your lies,
Is the resting place of pastors — the ghosts, whom you slander in the hereafter.
Thus, this perceived puritan past, which you cleave to with longing,
Has now become your personal haunting.
To some men, an accommodation, and others, a prohibition.
Let the "good-old souls," or demons you suppose, disclose the
Soiled fingers that grip the heavenly retribution
You're eager to throw,
Lest the stones in your hand turn to sand
In your itchy inquisition,
Lest another man dies."

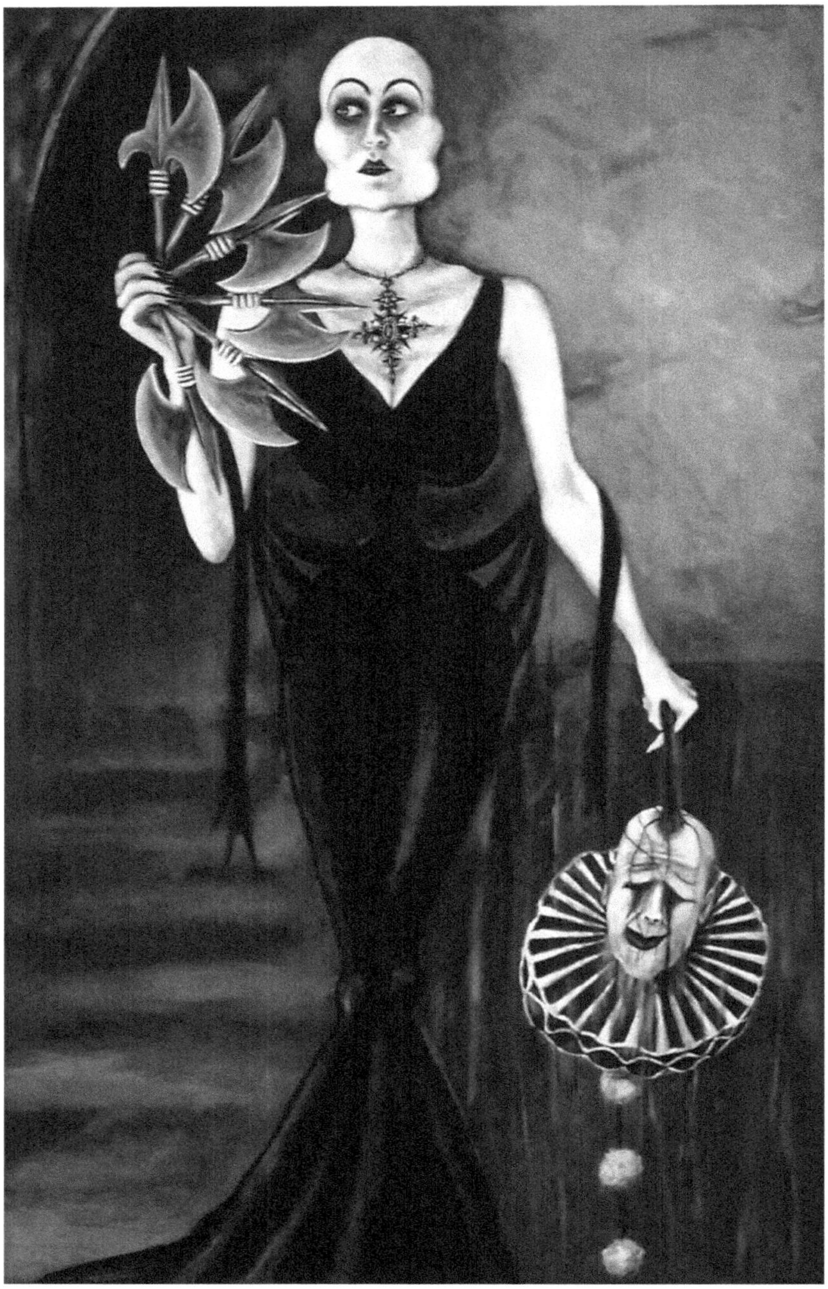

<u>BANZALTA DRAYN AND HER HATCHET-FAN PAIN</u>

O'er the mountain moors, and mouths mellowed with piercing ecstasy,
The toil of blood beasts decreases
As the debased beings forsake innocent cries of their feasting.
Fumes of its memory gave birth to Banzalta's accepting.
With impetus, she bathes in blood unprovoked.
Nocturnal habits burning.
Her pain-stained mouth feeds her veins, her parched vines,
Slicing the violets' throats,
Plunging deep as into vessels of fine wine.
Before the sun rises, she wraps herself in shrouds of sacred fabrics
And wipes her tears upon her fan of hatchets.

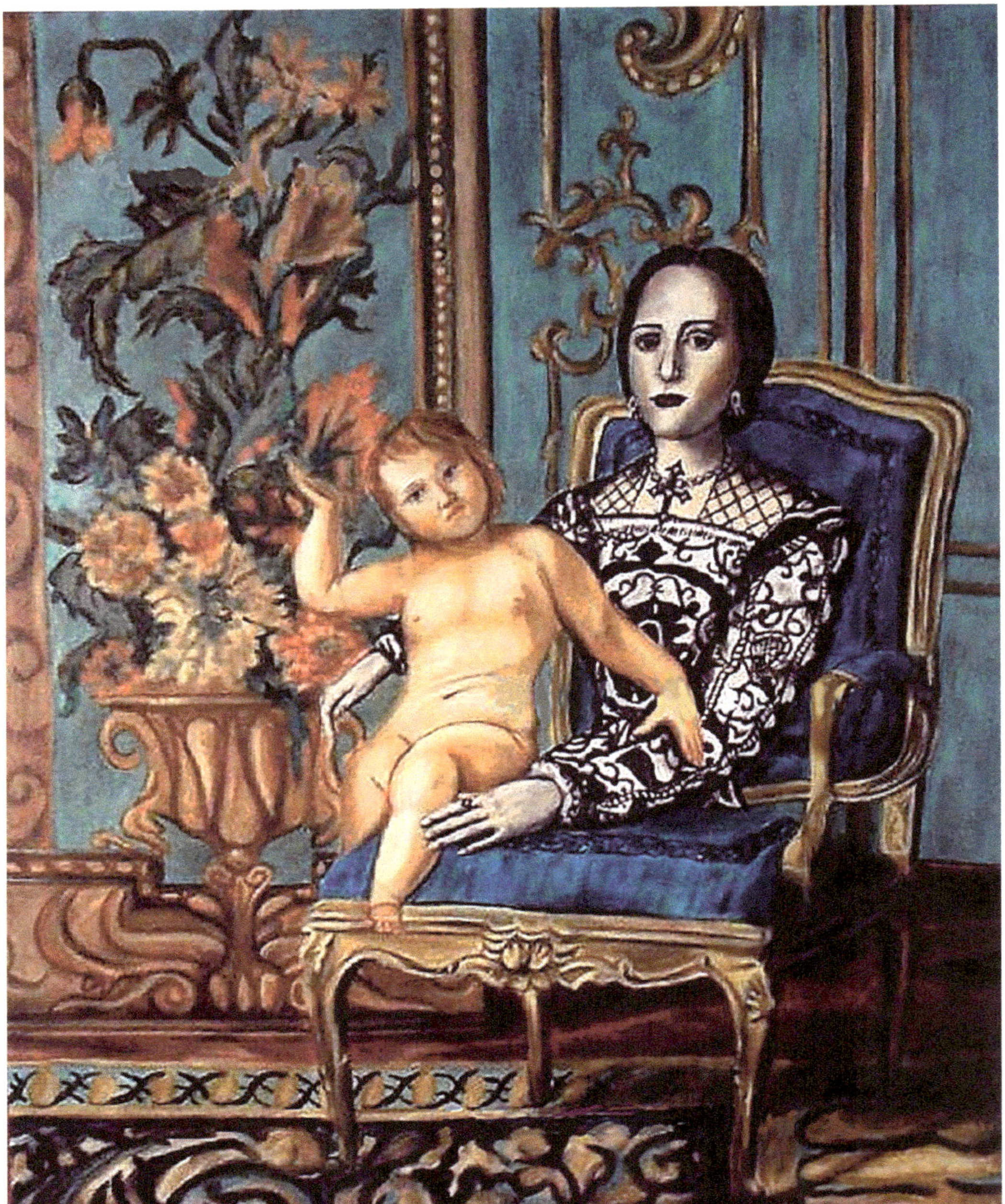

THE DEFEAT OF AMBERGIS

Ambergis is half the lady she once was
A pair of wings without the dove.
Her servants deserted her.
She destroyed her love.
Her only child, a giant, now resides
Across the great divide,
Which she unearthed from end to end,
With pious platitudes and virtuous mecca attitude,
In her depraved revenge.

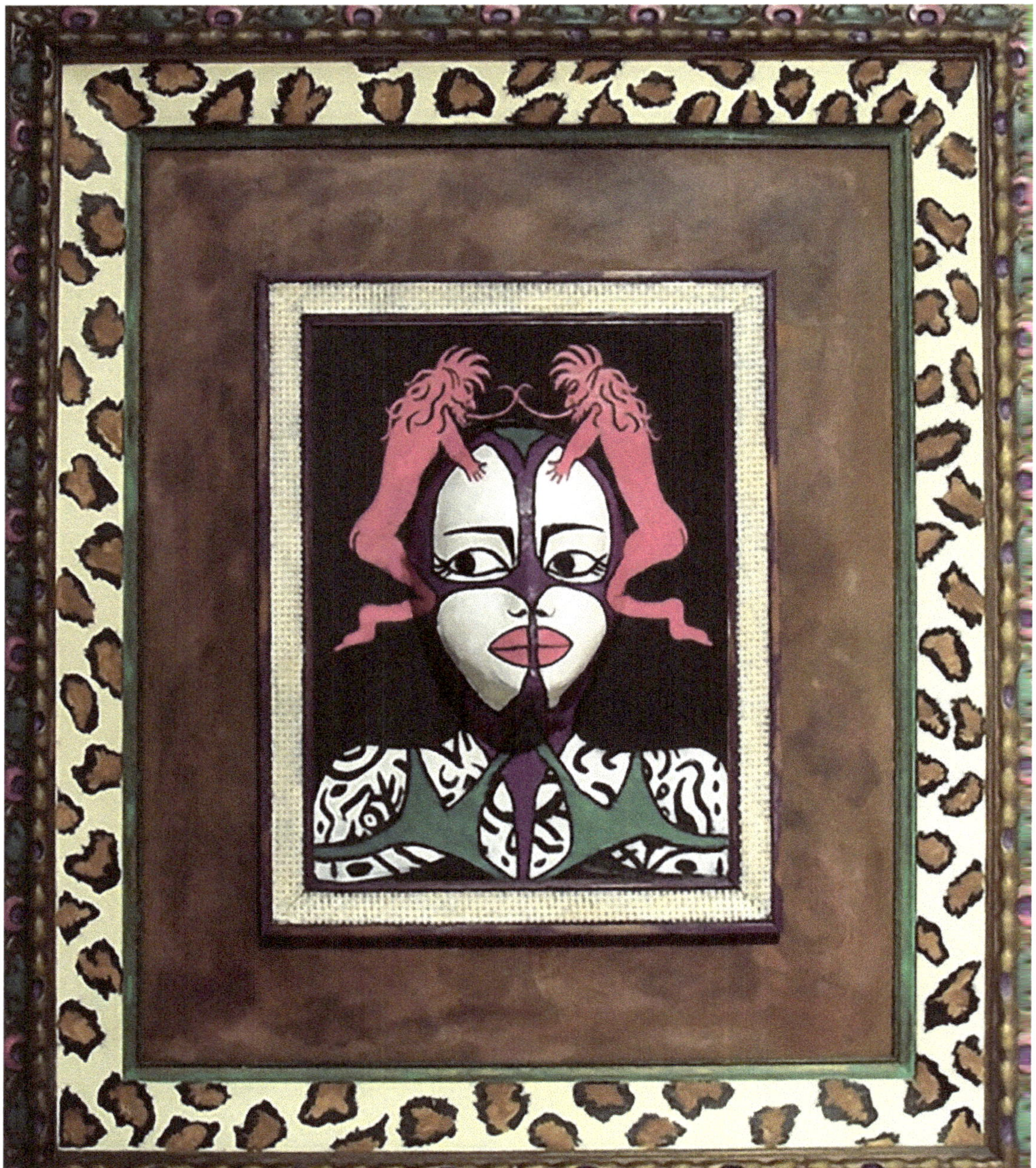

POSSESSED

Am I an author possessed?
Obsessed, oppressed the moment I dreamed of the Book of the Dead.
Hence, the cosmos often dictates my hand.
Automatic writing, unconscious calligraphy,
That started in a van in Denver when my parents went off the grid —
That first spring night.
I realized they had thrown away my life
With no definite plans.
My meager memoir was all that I had.
The cosmos, the guides, occasionally revisit
When I resist them using me as a mouthpiece.
Am I a reincarnation? I may never solve the puzzle.
But my pen must keep moving even though my mouth remains muzzled,
And the meaning of my writings may never be loud to me.

ABOUT THE AUTHOR

Milan Sergent studied creative writing in college and began writing the Candlewicke 13 novel series in 2007, a year after featuring some of the series' characters in his solo art exhibition, *Outsiders and Apparitions,* near Rockefeller Center in New York City.

Sergent's *Candlewicke 13 and the Tombstone Forest* won the Readers' Favorite Finalist Award in the Children - Fantasy/Sci-Fi category as well as the Book Excellence Award Finalist – Fantasy.

An artist and poet since adolescence, a few of Sergent's early poetic works were published in *Scarlet Literary Magazine.*

To learn more about the author and poet, visit **www.milansergent.com.** While there, join the mailing list for important news updates and notifications about future novel releases.

www.ingramcontent.com/pod-product-compliance
Ingram Content Group UK Ltd.
Pitfield, Milton Keynes, MK11 3LW, UK
UKHW060120010826
14089UKWH00005B/75

9 781734 877557